INSPIRED

CONTAINER

GARDENING

INSPIRED CONTAINER GARDENING

STEPHANIE DONALDSON
photographs by Juliette Wade

D&C
David and Charles

To Tim and William – JW

Inspired Container Gardening is based on an original idea by Juliette Wade

ACKNOWLEDGEMENTS

Stephanie Donaldson and Juliette Wade would like to thank Nick Wates for allowing his courtyard to be transformed into a corner of the Mediterranean, Nicola Bruce & Steve Pyke for letting us take photographs in their splendid conservatory and Jane King for her help looking after the plants. They would also like to thank Anna Mumford and the team at David & Charles for supporting the project from first idea to finished book. For this they owe special thanks to Michael Whitehead, the book designer and John Headford, the illustrator. Juliette Wade would like to thank Stephanie Donaldson for all her inspirational ideas, supportive influence, green fingers, hard work and wonderful text. Juliette would also like to thank all her family, friends and gardening acquaintances in Combe and elsewhere who have generously helped her with locations, plants, containers and props: Peter and Avice Clayton, Jean Wade, Diana and Richard Marsh, the Andrews, Di and Richard Woodward, Lallie and Andy Cox, Moira Booth, Connie Franks, Michel Green, Ian Howard, Edna and Don Hunt, George and Brigitte Speake, Gwen Bishop, Geoffrey Garton, Richard Sharp, Mr & Mrs Balmer, the staff at Daylesford House, Audrey Dyer, Christopher Gibbs, Janet Smith, the Harbour Inn at Southwold, the International Bulb Desk and Julia Malabre for her wonderful styling. Special thanks go to Tim and William Clayton for their loving support and for surrendering their garden to an army of containers.

PICTURE ACKNOWLEDGEMENTS
All photographs by Juliette Wade except for:
Pages 134 (top right) and 135 (far right) David Askham/Garden Picture Library; page 55 (bottom right) Mark Bolton/GPL; page 87 (top right) Lynne Britchie/GPL; pages 12 (right), 13 (bottom left), 68 (centre) and 103 (left) Chris Burrows/GPL; page 54 (bottom left and bottom right) Brian Carter/GPL; page 54 (top right) Densey Clyne/GPL; page 117 (top) Geoff Dann/GPL; page 116 (right) Christopher Fairweather/GPL; pages 12 (left), 13 (bottom right), 26 (top right and bottom right), 27 (left), 40 (top left and bottom right), 41 (right), 68 (bottom right), 69 (top right), 68, 87 (bottom right), 103 (centre right and far right), 116 (left), 117 (left), 134 (bottom left), 135 (centre left and centre right) and 150 (top) John Glover/GPL; page 116 (centre) Sunniva Harte/GPL; pages 13 (top left) and 69 (top left) Neil Holmes/GPL; page 55 (bottom left) Roger Hyam/GPL; page 54 (top left) Jacqui Hurst/GPL; page 135 (left) Lamontagne/GPL; page 117 (centre) A.I. Lord/GPL; pages 40 (bottom left), 68 (bottom left), 87 (bottom centre left) and 151 (bottom right) Jerry Pavia/GPL; pages 27 (right), 40 (top right), 41 (left), 87 (top left, bottom left and bottom centre left), 103 (centre left), 134 (top left) and 151 (bottom left, top left and top right) Howard Rice/GPL; pages 13 (top right), 26 (top left), 55 (top) and 134 (bottom right) J.S. Sira/GPL; page 150 (bottom) Tim Spence/GPL; page 69 (centre bottom) Friedrich Strauss/GPL; page 102 Didier Willery/GPL; page 26 (bottom left) Justyn Willsmore.

Illustrations on pages 11, 25, 39, 53, 67, 85, 101, 115, 133, 149, by John Headford

EDITOR'S NOTE
When making any of the projects in this book, follow either the
metric or the imperial dimensions – not a mixture of the two.

A DAVID & CHARLES BOOK
David & Charles is a subsidiary of F+W (UK) Ltd.,
an F+W Publications Inc. company

First published in 1999 as *Country Containers*
First paperback edition 2005

A catalogue record for this book is available from the British Library
ISBN 0 7153 2137 4

Printed in China by SNP Leefung
for David & Charles
Brunel House   Newton Abbot   Devon

Contents

Mediterranean

Conjure up a corner of Provence in your garden with brightly painted pots, dazzling flowers and fragrant herbs. Containers are perfect for many of the Mediterranean plants which thrive in hot, dry conditions and need a well-drained soil. Once they are established, these plants are undemanding and easy to grow.

EVEN IF YOU HAVE never visited the Mediterranean, the mention of it will certainly conjure up images in your head. Think of an azure sky, a turquoise sea, white-painted buildings and scarlet geraniums and you are instantly transported to one of the Greek islands. Picture red earth, stone terraces and hazy sunlight shining through the silver-grey foliage of olive trees onto deep purple lavender and flag iris and you have conjured up the view from the vine-shaded terrace of a Provençal farmhouse. The Mediterranean is a sensual landscape where everything seems to be more intense – colour, scent, sound and taste. Understandably, it is for many of us our dream landscape.

Inevitably, for some of us it will remain just that, but it is still possible to create an area in the garden which becomes your own little piece of the Mediterranean during the warm summer months. This might be on a tiny scale – perhaps an alcove in a wall painted a chalky sky blue in which you have placed a scarlet geranium in a terracotta pot – or a more ambitious scheme whereby the sunniest corner of your garden is transformed into a

typical Provençal terrace, with a dark green metal table and chairs under a vine-clad pergola, surrounded by pot-grown lemons, olives and oleanders – the perfect place to eat *al fresco* meals and enjoy the long summer evenings.

Although it is true that many of the plants we associate with the Mediterranean do require a true Mediterranean climate to thrive when planted directly into the soil, container-grown specimens are perfectly happy provided they are sheltered from the frost; even in Tuscany the lemons are brought under cover for the winter.

As the artists of the Impressionist and Fauve schools recognized, it is the quality of light in the Mediterranean which makes the region so special. Revelling in this light, the blue of the sea and the sky, the grey-green of the foliage, the hot colours of the flowers and the earth tones of ochre, umber and terracotta combine to create a unique palette.

LEFT: *A redundant cast-iron drain hopper is given the Mediterranean treatment when painted a bright, chalky blue and planted with red geraniums.*

RIGHT: *A seaside courtyard in southern England becomes Mediterranean by virtue of the clever use of paint colours and plants.*

Craft Project 1

PROVENÇAL PAINTED POTS

As WELL AS the better known terracotta, there is a long tradition in Provence of producing gorgeous glazed pots in rich colours. Some are glazed in a single colour, but the most appealing are underglazed yellow with a top glaze of green around the rim of the pot which is allowed to run down over the yellow. They are seldom available elsewhere, and if you do find them they tend to be prohibitively expensive. If you are really determined to buy one you could carry it home on your lap on the plane, but better still you can make excellent copies at home with a little bit of time and some gloss paint.

Method

1. Terracotta is very porous, so it is essential to seal the pot for a glossy finish. The easiest way to do this is to paint it initially with a coat of yellow paint diluted 50/50 with white spirit.

2. Allow to dry and then apply a second coat of undiluted yellow paint.

3. Once this is dry, add the green decoration. Starting at the rim, apply the green paint to the top quarter of the pot with a generously loaded brush. The paint will trickle down the pot, creating the desired effect.

1. Seal the pot with a coat of yellow paint, diluted 50/50 with white spirit. Leave to dry.

2. Apply a coat of undiluted yellow paint. Leave to dry.

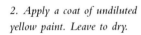

3. Load the brush with green paint and apply to the top of the pot, allowing the green paint to trickle down over the yellow paint.

Getting Good Results

Although the final effect achieved with these pots is very informal it isn't just a matter of slapping on the paint any old how – unless you are careful the pot may end up looking as if you simply got bored halfway through repainting it. You should also bear in mind that with a curved surface the drips may not always run straight down, but can veer off to one side as if you have decorated the pot in a high wind!

Choosing Colours

Yellows and greens come in so many tones it can be difficult to choose the right colours. A good guide to the colours used in this project is that they are based on the colours of a sunflower. (See Suppliers List on page 164 for paints.)

PELARGONIUMS

The pelargonium is the quintessential summer plant.
Amazingly colourful and easy to grow, it thrives in window
boxes, pots and hanging baskets, and will brighten the garden
from late spring to the first frosts.

Although the pelargonium is usually associated with southern Europe, where it fills the sun-baked courtyards and verandahs of Italy, France, Greece, Spain and Portugal, it has been grown in northern Europe for centuries. There are records of ivy-leaved pelargoniums growing in England as long ago as 1690.

Most pelargoniums have their origins in South Africa, where wild specimens were collected by plant hunters and brought to Europe over the centuries. Selective breeding and hybridization have created the many varieties we know today. The common name of 'geranium' by which many people know these plants is not technically wrong, as pelargoniums do belong to the Geraniaceae family, but using pelargonium does avoid confusion with the hardy geranium genus (*Geranium*).

There is a legend surrounding zonal pelargoniums (*Pelargonium zonale*) which recounts how long ago, on the shores of the Mediterranean, the prophet Mohammed washed his shirt and hung it to dry on a common mallow bush. When he returned the mallow had been transformed into a striking pelargonium. Myth or not, the zonal pelargonium has very distinctive markings with a circular band of bronze or deep red near the margins of the leaves.

TYPES OF PELARGONIUM

There are four distinctive types of pelargonium: zonal, regal, ivy-leaved and species, the last of which includes the varieties with scented foliage.

ZONAL PELARGONIUMS

The zonal pelargonium is the variety we think of as the bedding geranium with its single or double flowers. There are literally hundreds of hybrids to choose from in colours that range from clean, vibrant reds to pure whites or apple-blossom pinks. With their rigid stems and umbrella-shaped leaves, they will quickly fill a terracotta pot to create a splash of colour wherever they are placed. Planted individually, each plant will need a 15cm (6in) pot, while a 30cm (12in) pot will hold three plants. They look best when only one variety is planted in each container, and for smaller pots the dwarf varieties which reach less than 30cm (12in) are a good choice. Zonals are sometimes grown as standards from cuttings taken in the summer and grown indoors through the winter.

Today there is an increasingly wide range of unusual zonal pelargoniums available. Some have variegated foliage and others have particularly vivid zonal markings. Generally the flowers are less dominant than in the traditional varieties, and they are often carried on long, delicate stems well above the foliage. They are an ideal choice for someone who wants to create a subtler effect. 'Distinction' is a particularly good variety with its chocolate-brown zonal markings and brilliant scarlet flowers.

REGAL PELARGONIUMS

Regal pelargoniums are hybrids of several pelargonium species and have a shrubby, upright appearance with large, showy flowers. They were great favourites in Victorian and Edwardian England, when they were used in conservatory displays and as houseplants. They are sometimes known as 'show geraniums' and the flowers, which are often frilly, two-toned

Pelargonium 'Mrs Quilter'

Pelargonium 'Deacon Mandarin'

extravaganzas, are highly prized by flower show *aficionados*. *En masse* they are rather too contrived for the country look, but an individual pot placed in a group of flowering plants has an old-fashioned charm. Although regal pelargoniums have been rather out of fashion in the recent past, they are now enjoying a resurgence of popularity. Two varieties which are recommended are 'Lord Bute', with dark maroon flowers with cerise margins to the petals, and 'Voodoo', with intense cerise flowers and maroon markings on the petals. The regal pelargonium is less tolerant of poor weather than the other varieties and rain will mark the flowers, but regular feeding and dead-heading will ensure that when the weather is good the flowers will look their best.

IVY-LEAVED PELARGONIUMS

The ivy-leaved pelargonium (*Pelargonium peltatum*) is the best choice for window boxes and hanging baskets, where its naturally

Pelargonium 'Fringed Aztec'

Growing Pelargoniums

Pelargoniums like full sun and well-drained potting compost – ideally a mix of 50/50 standard potting compost with loam-based compost and added coarse grit for drainage. Pelargoniums can be combined with other plants or grown on their own, and will need regular watering and dead-heading and feeding fortnightly with a high-potassium feed (tomato fertilizer is ideal). Many people discard their pelargoniums at the end of the season, but they can be nurtured over winter if kept quite dry and frost-free. Cut them back by half when bringing them under cover and take cuttings from new shoots in the early spring.

Pelargonium 'Peach'

Pelargonium 'Lord Bute'

trailing habit can be seen to best advantage. The stems can grow to 1m (3¹/₄ft). The leaves are similar in shape to those of the ivy and the loose flower umbels give the plant a more relaxed appearance than either the zonals or the regals. Colours tend to be softer too, in shades of pink, white and cream, although there are named varieties in deep maroon, red and mauve. One of the most delicate is *P.* 'L'Elégante', the flowers of which are barely pink, complemented by

pretty leaves edged in white, often with a pink flush.

The most popular Continental varieties, known as 'balcon' pelargoniums, tend to be in stronger colours such as 'Decora Impérial', one of the most widely grown scarlet pelargoniums in Europe, and the old favourite 'Ville de Paris', with deep rose-pink flowers. The secret to achieving the Mediterranean look with ivy-leaved pelargoniums is to grow several plants of the same variety

in a basket or box (individually the plants can look very uninspiring) and allow them to tumble down the face of the building.

SPECIES PELARGONIUMS

Species pelargoniums, particularly the scented-leaved varieties, have long been cottage-garden favourites. Planted in terracotta pots they spend the summer months in the garden near the kitchen door, where brushing against them releases their scent, before being brought indoors to the kitchen windowsill for the winter. Their leaves can be used to scent pot-pourris and even give a delicious flavour to cakes and custards. A collection of scented pelargoniums will reveal the breadth and variety of scents available, from the well-known lemon-scented variety (*P. crispum*) to the less common, including *P.* 'Attar of Roses', *P. tomentosum,* which smells of peppermint, and the beautifully variegated and fragrant *P.* 'Lady Plymouth'.

Pelargonium 'Caligula'

If you are fortunate enough to visit Tuscany or Provence and walk in the rocky hills you quickly become aware that you are surrounded by aromatic herbs growing in the most unpromising of situations; a wild thyme emerges from a crevice in the rocks, a shrubby rosemary tumbles over a neglected terrace and silver-leaved sage finds a foothold in a little pocket of soil next to a path. Ironically, despite our best endeavours the much-pampered herbs which we grow at home often seem to struggle to survive.

To grow Mediterranean herbs successfully you need to give them conditions as close as possible to those they would enjoy naturally. In other words, they need to be in full sun, in free-draining soil which is not too rich, and they should not be overwatered. Terracotta or stone pots or troughs are ideal containers for this type of plant; plastic is not as good as it tends to retain moisture and does not hold warmth the way the other materials do.

Ideally, the herbs should be planted in a loam-based compost with about one-third added coarse grit for additional drainage. If the herbs have been commercially grown in a peat-based compost you will need to soak the plant and gently loosen the rootball when transplanting or the roots will find it difficult to make their way into the loam from the peat. Peat can form a water-resistant plug that seals the plant off from its surroundings, and this is one of the most common reasons for losing plants whether they are transplanted into containers or into the garden. As with all types of plants, transplanting is best done in the cool of the evening or early morning and, once settled into their new surroundings, the plants should be thoroughly watered. A mulch of coarse grit or gravel on top of the soil will look good, help retain moisture and prevent soil splashing onto the leaves during heavy rain or watering. Although plants which are native to the Mediterranean can survive in very dry conditions, this does not mean that they should not be watered, but it does mean that they prefer light watering and, with the exception of basil, will do better without a saucer under the pot.

Herbs should always be planted where they are easily accessible from the kitchen: romantic thoughts of drifting down to the bottom of the garden and gathering a basket of fresh herbs are unlikely to be as appealing in the pouring rain or in the middle of winter. Group pots of herbs on a tabletop on the terrace, next to the kitchen door, on a windowsill or alongside a path – somewhere you can brush against them and release their fragrance as you pass by. Many herbs are evergreen and will make an attractive display all year round, especially if they are planted in pots of different shapes and sizes. A standard rosemary looks wonderful in a plain terracotta pot, especially when it is underplanted with creeping thymes.

Larger thymes, prostrate rosemaries and sages like to tumble down the sides of urns and this too makes a striking display.

You will find there are many varieties of each herb and choosing the best one can be tricky. Ideally you should select varieties which combine good culinary qualities with decorative foliage and flowers – for instance, *Salvia officinalis* 'Icterina' with green and gold variegated foliage and *S. o.* 'Purpurascens' (purple-leaved sage) are more eye-catching than the usual silver-leaved form. The foliage and flowers of rosemary can vary enormously; for clear, deep-blue flowers choose *Rosmarinus officinalis* 'Tuscan Blue' or *R. o.* 'Severn Sea', while *R. o.* 'Miss Jessopp's Upright' has tall, strong, upright growth. Recommended thymes include the golden-leaved lemon thyme *Thymus × citriodorus* 'Archer's Gold' and the variegated *T. × citriodorus* 'Silver Queen'. Although they are not strictly culinary thymes, the creeping thymes are wonderfully fragrant and their carpets of colourful flowers should be included in any herb display – look out for *T. serpyllum* 'Annie Hall', *T. s.* 'Pink Chintz' and *T. plicata* 'Doone Valley'. Culinary marjoram and oregano are cultivars of the wild varieties and are not particularly decorative, but they are still worth growing as they are essential flavourings in Mediterranean food and are much loved by bees.

Many of the best loved and most familiar Mediterranean plants, including lemon, olive and oleander, make excellent container plants, and contrary to popular belief they do not need to be kept in a heated greenhouse or conservatory over winter, although some do need to be kept frost-free.

The lemon tree is a perfect example. There is a long tradition of growing lemons and other citrus fruit in containers which are stood outside during the spring, summer and autumn months and then moved under cover for the winter. You can still see orangeries in the grounds of many of the grand houses of Europe, with tall arched windows to ensure good light to keep the trees in leaf all year. The original Versailles tubs were designed to hold the citrus trees which graced the parterres and terraces of the palace of Versailles. These straight-sided wooden boxes had metal rings on each side through which poles could be threaded so that the large trees could be moved in and out of the orangeries more easily.

However, you need neither an orangery nor a Versailles tub to grow citrus trees. A sheltered, sunny corner during the summer combined with a frost-free shed, porch or greenhouse for winter will suffice. *Citrus × meyeri* 'Meyer' (Meyer's Lemon) is the most commonly cultivated variety for container-growing and it will bear lemons from an early age. This is a plant which prefers to be under-potted – in other words it likes its roots to be fairly restricted – and it should be moved into a larger pot only when it becomes seriously pot-bound. A loam-based compost suitable for shrubs and trees such as John Innes No. 3 is the best growing medium. Place a good layer of rotted manure in the base of the pot before planting the tree and mulch with a further layer on top of the soil. Water thoroughly when transplanting. Lemons prefer a thorough soaking once a week rather than a light daily watering. Commercial citrus growers have found that the best feed for their pot-grown trees is slow-release fertilizer granules sprinkled on the surface of the compost in the spring. This will last for six months. Foliar feeding is also beneficial, especially when the tree is producing a flush of new leaves and flowers.

Although a lemon tree can tolerate light frost, it should be brought under cover before cold, wet weather sets in. Stand it in a light position, without a saucer under the pot, and water sparingly. It will probably drop many of its leaves and may also have a flush of flowers and some new leaf growth before becoming semi-dormant for the winter. Watch out for scale insect, the major citrus pest – the scales will be seen under the leaves and at the leaf joints. Use malathion fortnightly to control it.

A Provençal theme is established by combining exotic-looking architectural plants with pot-grown lemons, olives and oleanders.

Compared with the citrus family, other Mediterranean shrubs and trees are not quite so demanding, and in fact some positively thrive on a bit of benign neglect. Like the citrus, all will grow best in a loam-based compost such as John Innes No. 3 with a layer of composted manure in the base of the pot and an annual topdressing with more manure.

Olive trees make very successful container plants: they only need repotting once every five years, are tolerant of some frost and will even bear olives! Think of the natural habitat of the olive and you will realize that it is not a demanding plant – it will grow in very poor soil and needs little water to survive. However, it is also true that growing in these conditions is a slow process and if you haven't got a couple of centuries to spare, your tree will grow faster if fed and watered regularly. In frost-free regions, the olive can be kept outside all year provided it is in a warm, sheltered spot, but in colder regions it should be brought under cover during the winter.

The oleander (*Nerium oleander*) is a beautiful shrub with showy flowers in shades of pink, red, white, cream and even yellow. After flowering, the stems which have borne the flowers should be cut back to near the base. The oleander only flowers on new growth. Wear gloves when pruning this plant, as the sap is poisonous; in fact, all parts of the plant are poisonous and it is not recommended for a garden which is used by small children.

Drive along the coast of Provence in February and the hillsides will be yellow with the flowers of mimosa (*Acacia dealbata*). In the south of France this is the quintessential spring flower just as the daffodil is in northern countries. If you live in a mild region you can leave your mimosa outside all year, but in other areas it will need some frost protection. As this is a plant which flowers very early in the year it is best kept in a porch or conservatory where you will be able to admire its fragrant flowers. Later in the year its feathery foliage will be a good backdrop to various Mediterranean plants.

Other typically Mediterranean plants which are easy to cultivate and essential to have if you wish to turn your garden into a corner of Provence or Tuscany are lavender, agapanthus and arum lily.

Lavender comes in many varieties and colours; although the deep colours make the most impact, some of the more unusual varieties such as tender *Lavandula dentata* and *L. pinnata* have lovely flowers and soft, feathery, highly aromatic foliage, while French lavender (*L. stoechas*) has extraordinary tufted flowers. Lavenders should be planted in the same way as other aromatic Mediterranean herbs.

Agapanthus and arum lilies will do well in pots, especially when planted in a rich compost with plenty of added manure. Agapanthus flowers best in full

ABOVE: *Glazed olive and white Spanish pots filled with vivid pink geraniums are reminiscent of the courtyards of Córdoba.*

LEFT: *A collection of lavenders surround an olive tree which has grown happily in its pot for the past 20 years.*

sun, but arum lily (*Zantedeschia aethiopica*) prefers partial shade.

In its natural habitat the arum lily is a marginal plant growing along streams in boggy soil. It will grow best in a container when stood in a deep, water-filled saucer, or better still, plunged up to the pot rim in a pond.

Creating a Mediterranean garden is not simply about choosing the right plants, although this is an important element. As with all good design, colour, shape and form should be considered and applied to different aspects of the garden – the hard landscaping, the furniture, the pots, the location, and the plants themselves. On a bright summer's day it may be that your garden can take on some of the characteristics of southern Europe, but it must work on dull, wet days as well, so it may be necessary to make some compromises. A seaside garden in a sunny coastal location can use the bright, hot colours of the Mediterranean palette on walls and woodwork. Lots of white paint, highlighted with deep blues and turquoises, makes an ideal backdrop for vibrant, tumbling geraniums. Even on a dull day the quality of light at the seaside is such that these colours will not look inappropriate. In cooler, cloudier climates it is emulating this light which is the most elusive aspect of creating a Mediterranean garden and a more northerly location will do better to use a softer, warm palette. It is still possible to evoke a corner of Provence by using mauves, lavenders, soft whites, grey-greens and dark greens. Woodwork painted grey or lavender looks wonderful against weathered stone or brick, and while pots of lavenders, artemisias and sage set around the base of a standard rosemary, bay or olive will be deliciously

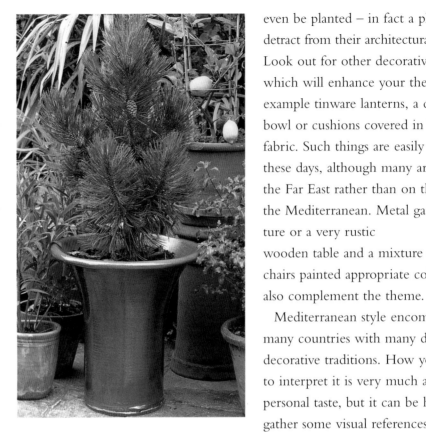

fragrant on a hot day, their subtle beauty will still appeal under a cloudy sky.

Look at any pictures of Mediterranean gardens and you will see that the materials used are often very different to those we use in our gardens. Re-creating a Mediterranean garden with authentic materials can be an expensive business, so this is a time for compromise. Accept that your brick or stone walls or paths will never look typically Provençal and concentrate on the planting, as tumbling herbs and cleverly grouped pots will soon disguise these surfaces. Use mass-produced, easily obtainable pots for most of your plants, and invest in a couple of beautiful Cretan pots to use as focal points. The special pots need not

even be planted – in fact a plant may detract from their architectural beauty. Look out for other decorative objects which will enhance your theme, for example tinware lanterns, a carved stone bowl or cushions covered in Provençal fabric. Such things are easily obtainable these days, although many are made in the Far East rather than on the shores of the Mediterranean. Metal garden furniture or a very rustic wooden table and a mixture of old chairs painted appropriate colours will also complement the theme.

Mediterranean style encompasses many countries with many different decorative traditions. How you choose to interpret it is very much a matter of personal taste, but it can be helpful to gather some visual references, so take lots of pictures when you are on holiday and tear out pictures from magazines and holiday brochures – it's amazing how helpful this can be.

Try not to get carried away in an attempt to encompass all aspects of Mediterranean style in your garden, or the result will look muddled and lacking in theme. Instead, choose your favourite style, be it Spanish courtyard, Tuscan farmhouse or Greek taverna, and select paint colours, containers and plants accordingly.

ABOVE: **Pinus mugo** *is a slow-growing pine which warrants a fine pot in which it can mature into a magnificent specimen.*

RIGHT: *Sometimes a pot has such inherent beauty that plants would be a distraction.*

American Country

Firmly rooted in the rural traditions

of the early settlers, American Country

style is inspired by the simple furniture,

implements and quilts of the Shaker,

Amish and New England communities.

Flowers from the Old and New worlds

mingle in colourful displays.

THE ESSENCE OF American Country style can be found in the containers themselves: rough-hewn troughs, functional wooden boxes, woven baskets, tinware and simple terracotta pots. Life was hard for the early settlers and their possessions were few; apart from what they had brought with them from their country of origin, everything they owned was either made by their own hands or traded with neighbours. It is this functional simplicity combined with creative recycling and gentle decoration which inspires the planting in this chapter.

The earliest settlers' gardens were used almost exclusively to grow food and medicinal plants. Plants were grown because they were useful, not because they were beautiful, from seeds which the settlers had brought with them from Europe. Many of the traditional cottage-garden flowers were essential ingredients for the folk medicine on which each family would rely for health and well-being. As life became more settled and peaceful there was time to explore the surrounding countryside in search of useful plants and to learn about the medicinal plants of the Native Americans, so gradually indigenous plants were

introduced alongside those grown from imported seeds. The Shakers in particular were skilful gardeners who developed a profitable trade in medicinal plants. They were renowned for the quality and purity of their herbs and although they were not allowed to cultivate 'useless' flowers, many plants which were beautiful as well as useful were grown in their gardens.

Today's American Country garden is a blend of the Old World and the New. Many of the plants which were originally introductions have now been in America for over 400 years; they have become naturalized and are as much a part of the landscape as they are in Europe. Similarly, plants collected in America and brought back to Europe by intrepid plant hunters have become commonplace in the gardens of England and elsewhere.

RIGHT: *A Shaker-style woven basket, planted with* **Bellis** *daisies, makes an attractive window box.*

LEFT: *Echoing the distinctive chequerboard patterning of* Fritillaria meleagris, *a terracotta pot is stencilled with a gingham-effect heart. The heart-shape is first stencilled rust-red, then, with the template still in place, vertical stripes are formed using strips of masking tape. White paint is stippled over the exposed areas and left to dry. The tape is peeled off before repeating the process with horizontal stripes which will complete the checked design.*

Craft Project 2

AMERICAN COUNTRY TROUGH

YOU WILL NEED
- Rough-hewn timber boards 15mm (⅝in) thick, cut to dimensions given opposite
- Stiff card for template
- Electric or hand saw
- Jigsaw
- Hammer
- Block plane
- 50mm (2in) nails
- Waterproof woodglue
- Electric sander or sandpaper
- Electric or hand drill and large drill-bit

For wall hanging:
- Masonry bit
- Screwdriver
- 2 x 50mm (2in) x No.10 roundhead screws
- Wall plugs
- 2 x 200mm (8in) angle brackets and screws

THE ESSENCE OF Shaker style is simplicity, and this trough fits the bill exactly. This example is made from boards which are 15mm (⅝in) thick, but thicker timber would work.

Construction

1. Cut the base, side, front and back panels to the dimensions given opposite. (Glue and nail a narrow strip to the *bottom* edge of the back and front to make up the width, if necessary.)
2. Draw a circle 175mm (7in) in diameter onto card using compasses or a plate. Use this to mark out the curves on the front and back.
3. Cut out the curves with a jigsaw, working into the

angles from both directions.
4. Assemble by glueing and nailing the front and back to the sides so the bottom edges are flush. Turn the trough upside down, glue and nail the base in position, and plane the edges to match the angled sides. Sand down any rough edges and drill 4–5 drainage holes in the base.
5. This trough can be wall-hung by drilling two holes in the back (see opposite). Drill the wall and fit wall plugs, then screw in the roundhead screws until the heads are 15mm (⅝in) from the wall. Support the weight of the trough by screwing angle brackets to the wall beneath it. See the panel opposite for advice on finishing.

TO DECORATE
- Water-based exterior wood stain
- Paintbrush
- Stencil
- Stencil brush
- Masking tape
- Matt acrylic varnish
- Soft clean cloth

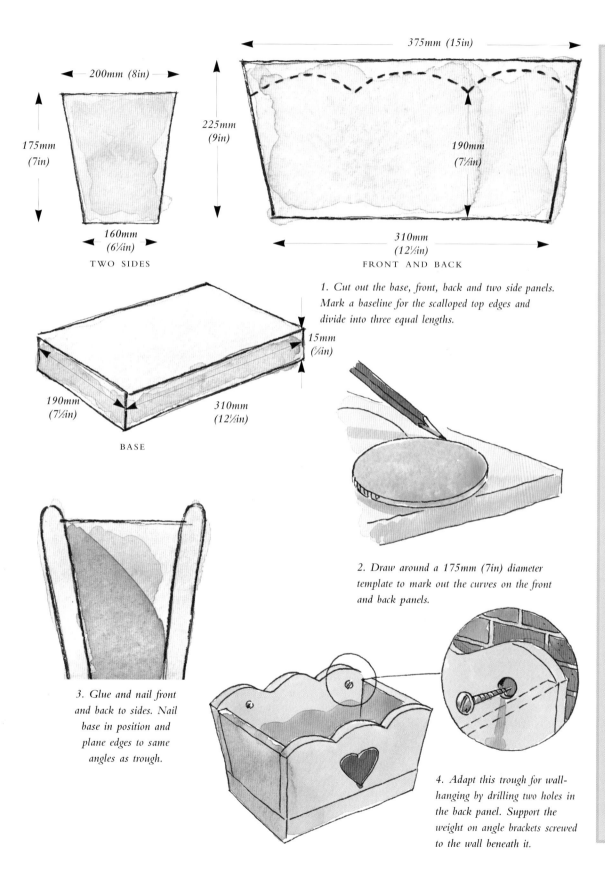

200mm (8in)

175mm (7in)

225mm (9in)

160mm (6¼in)

TWO SIDES

375mm (15in)

190mm (7½in)

310mm (12½in)

FRONT AND BACK

15mm (⅝in)

190mm (7½in)

310mm (12½in)

BASE

1. Cut out the base, front, back and two side panels. Mark a baseline for the scalloped top edges and divide into three equal lengths.

2. Draw around a 175mm (7in) diameter template to mark out the curves on the front and back panels.

3. Glue and nail front and back to sides. Nail base in position and plane edges to same angles as trough.

4. Adapt this trough for wall-hanging by drilling two holes in the back panel. Support the weight on angle brackets screwed to the wall beneath it.

Stencilling

Fix a heart-shaped stencil on the trough with masking tape. Using a lightly loaded stencil brush, stipple the design in a contrasting colour, using emulsion or acrylic paint diluted to the consistency of thick cream. Carefully remove the stencil and leave to dry. To make the stencil more muted, apply a second coat of wood stain over the stencil design and immediately wipe over with a cloth.

Staining and Decorating

Use a wood stain formulated for garden use; this allows the grain of the wood to show through but still acts as a preservative, and does not harm plants. Before painting, lightly sand the wood to remove any old paint or varnish. Paint on the stain following the grain of the wood. Leave to dry for 15 minutes and then wipe a soft cloth over the surface to remove excess paint and reveal more of the grain.

MINIATURE BULBS

*Miniature bulbs are perfect spring plants for gardeners
with limited space, especially when they can be viewed at
eye level, grown in a small window box or in small
pots grouped on steps.*

Fritillaria meleagris

FRITILLARIA

The small nodding bells of the smaller fritillaries are visually ideal for late spring containers and most species will adapt well to containers. Although the common snake's head fritillary (*Fritillaria meleagris*) can be grown in pots, the bulbs will need to be kept moist through the summer. There are however plenty of interesting alternatives that like a fertile but free-draining soil and won't need to be watered so carefully. The following varieties will grow happily in a mixture of one part horticultural grit to two parts loam-based potting compost. If possible plant in late summer, or early autumn at the latest, setting the bulbs 10cm (4in) deep. Protect the containers from heavy rain and cover the soil with a layer of coarse grit.

F. *affinis* is one of the easiest fritillaries to grow in a container, despite the exotic appearance given by its patterned petals. It enjoys a position in dappled shade, but can tolerate periods of drying out. F. *affinis* is up to 60cm (24in) tall, but the miniature form *F.a.* var. *tristulis* reaches only 20cm (8in) high. F. *michailovskyi* is a delightful multi-headed plant, 10–15cm (4–6in) high, with striking purple bells edged with golden yellow. It flowers from late spring to early summer, likes a position in full sun and can stand some drying out in summer. Not as widely available but well worth growing is F. *hermonis* subsp. *amana*, a short-stemmed fritillary 12.5cm (5in) high which grows happily in containers and has the most unusual lime-green and purple striped petals.

Fritillary bulbs can be expensive to buy, especially the less common

Fritillaria michailovskyi

Tulipa tarda

Narcissus 'Jack Snipe'

cultivars, so it is well worth increasing the stock you already have. After the bulbs have been in situ for a few years they will stop producing as many flowers, and this is the time to lift and divide them. Wait until the flowers have finished and the leaves are just beginning to change colour, then knock them out of the pot onto a sheet of plastic. Remove the compost and divide the clumps into single bulbs. Replant the bulbs immediately in a similar mixture of one part horticultural grit to two parts compost.

TULIPA

Miniature tulips have a charm and elegance that their larger cousins sometimes lack. Most of the miniature or small-flowered tulips are named cultivars or hybrids of the species tulips. They enjoy a well-drained compost and should be planted in autumn about 10cm (4in) deep. Species tulips like a sunny position and can either be left in pots through the summer or lifted for replanting in the autumn. *Tulipa praestans* 'Fusilier' is 15cm (6in) high and has flame-red flowers against soft green foliage. Each bulb produces a cluster of two to four blooms. Another good red is *T. maximowiczii*, which has single flowers about 15cm (6in) high. The crocus tulip (*T. humilis* var. *pulchella* 'Violet Queen') produces goblet-shaped flowers on stems up to 10cm (4in) high. The flowers are a bright violet pink and appear towards the end of winter. *T. tarda* is a tiny yellow and

Iris reticulata 'George'

Cultivation

Use terracotta flowerpots which allow the compost to 'breathe' and prevent waterlogging. Glazed pots can aggravate the problem, as can plant saucers if used during winter. Protect the pots from prolonged downpours of rain, particularly in the autumn; if necessary move the pots under cover for the winter and return to the open for the spring. If the bulbs are left in a container for more than a year they will need some additional feeding. When the foliage has unfurled in the spring, use a dilute high-potash fertilizer such as a tomato feed. For a good show of flowers, plant the bulbs close together but not touching. Plant in groups of three, five or seven, as this always looks better than even numbers.

creamy-white tulip whose flowers open out fully to give a star-like appearance. They grow no higher than 4 in (10cm) and appear in mid-spring.

NARCISSUS

Dwarf narcissi or daffodils make a delightful easy-to-grow subject for pots. The best-known varieties are the early-flowering *Narcissus* 'February Gold' and the petite *N.* 'Tête-à-tête', both 20–25cm (8–10in) high. 'Jack Snipe' has a deep yellow trumpet with a ruff of white outer petals. *N. bulbocodium*, better known as hoop-petticoat narcissus, is unusual and pretty, with short flared trumpets and narrow grass-like leaves. Plant in early autumn 15cm (6in) deep in well-drained multi-purpose compost. Narcissi thrive in sun or light shade and can be left in

position throughout the summer or lifted and stored until autumn.

IRIS

Dwarf irises provide some of the richest colours of all spring bulbs and the miniature types are ideal for pots. They flower early in the year well before most daffodils and tulips. The two main groups are *Iris reticulata* and *I. histrioides*, both of which grow to a height of 10cm (4in) and flower in late winter. Irises prefer a sharply drained compost (mixed with horticultural grit) and a sunny or partly shaded position. Plant the bulbs 5cm (2in) deep in groups of five or more.

I. 'Harmony', a Reticulata, is a hardy bulb which bears flowers of a deep, inky blue with yellow and white markings on the falls. *I.* 'Katherine Hodgkin' (Reticulata) is an interesting hybrid in soft

bluish-green with yellow and dark maroon markings. The tiniest iris of all is *I. danfordiae*, a deep yellow species only 8cm (3in) high.

SCILLA & PUSCHKINIA

Better known as squills, these bulbs have bell-shaped flowers and strap-like leaves (the common bluebell, now *Hyacinthoides non-scripta*, was formerly classed as *Scilla*). The miniature versions are widely grown in alpine and rock gardens and make very neat subjects for containers. *Puschkinia scilloides* has baby-blue flowers with a distinctive darker blue stripe running down the centre of the petals. *Scilla mischtschenkoana* has more open, star-shaped flowers in the palest silver and also has a faint stripe on the petals. *S. siberica* is bright azure blue. All three plants reach a height of 10cm (4in), ideal for windowledges, walls and tabletops. Plant the bulbs in late summer in multi-purpose compost, about 7.5cm (3in) deep.

Puschkinia scilloides

Simple containers and informal planting are central to American Country style, and while a faded wooden cabin may be the perfect setting for this type of planting, it can also add character to a garden shed, barn or outhouse, especially if the building itself has been embellished with some appropriate decorative touches. Clever styling can transform a utilitarian area of the garden into an eye-catching asset. A slightly rickety potting shed at the end of the garden, for example, can be redeveloped by covering the felt roof with sheets of corrugated iron, pinning some simple

check gingham curtains at the window and hanging decorative tinware from its weathered timber to create your very own settler's cabin ready and waiting for some American Country planting.

Making a utilitarian building look more attractive should not mean that it becomes less useful; in fact you will probably find that inspired by the improvement in its external appearance you will be motivated to sort out the inside as well, in the course of which you may well find yet more bits and pieces which you can recycle into useful and attractive containers and decorative accessories!

Boxes and troughs can be made with recycled timber, partly for economics, but also to stay in keeping with the settlers' principles of making good use of all materials. It is not necessary to visit folk-art shops and buy expensive replicas; follow the example of the settlers and look around you for what can be retrieved and reused. You should be able to find nearly everything you want secondhand. The exception might be decorative tinware, which can be very expensive if it is genuinely old, but new plain or punched tinware is quite cheap and widely available and will quickly weather down to resemble the antique equivalent.

Your own attic or cellar, jumble sales, charity shops and junkyards are excellent sources of chipped cooking pots, well-worn baskets and old terracotta pots, all of which make

charming and appropriate containers. Vine trimmings from the garden can be twisted into pretty garlands or heart shapes and hung from nails. Old garden implements, long past their useful life, still look good propped next to a doorway, while a discarded wicker bicycle basket hung under the eaves is a perfect place to keep your hand tools.

Although some of the early settlers would not have approved of decoration for its own sake, there were certain motifs, such as the heart and the tulip, which became increasingly popular. This form of decoration was introduced by the Pennsylvania Dutch and was based on the folk art traditions of their native land. The tulip in particular was a favourite decorative device; the settlers had brought bulbs of this much-prized flower with them to the New World, possibly because it had religious significance for these deeply devout people. The species tulip, often with three flowerheads on a stem, was considered to represent the Holy Trinity and in 16th-century Germany, where many of the immigrants originated, the tulip was considered to be a version of the Holy Lily.

LEFT: *A heart-decorated pot filled with 'Angélique' tulips combines a folk art pattern used by the Pennsylvania Dutch with the bulbs they brought to America from the Old World.*

RIGHT: *A discarded tin pot has real 'pioneer' character. Planted with blue* Anemone nemerosa, *it looks wonderful hung on a weathered shed wall. A simple vine heart completes the picture.*

Making your own American Country-style containers does not mean that you need the skill of a Shaker craftsman; the pared-down beauty of their workmanship was the result of a lifetime's dedication to the craft of furniture-making and a long way from the rough-hewn pieces made by the early settlers. What they had in common was simplicity of form. Every piece of timber the settlers used, unless it was recycled, involved cutting down a tree and hand-sawing the planks, and every nail used was individually forged by the blacksmith. Consequently, if a box or shelf was needed it would use the minimum of materials in the most straightforward way. Bear this in mind when making your boxes, troughs or window boxes as it will help you to achieve an authentic-looking result.

Nowadays we sometimes lose sight of the fact that paint's main function is as a protective coating. Early pieces would have been painted solely to prolong their life and paint would have been a scarce commodity, but as life became easier and supplies more plentiful the settlers had the time and the materials to add embellishments. The first American paints were milk paints, which used milk to bind pigments derived from plants, minerals and clays. Their opaque finish and muted colours are typical of the paints used by the Shakers and some American paint companies are now

RIGHT: *Here the star pattern on the window box is echoed by the star-like flowers of blue* Anemone blanda.

BELOW: *Stencilled motifs enliven weathered terracotta pots which are planted with vivid red tulip 'Red Riding Hood'.*

manufacturing them once more. However, it is not necessary to buy historically accurate paints; in keeping with the settlers' philosophy of wasting nothing you can use left-over emulsion, eggshell or satinwood paints, though gloss paint is not recommended. Water-based paints may be thinned down by adding water, and oil-based paints can be thinned with white spirit. Thinning down will allow the grain of the wood to show through more clearly. If the colours are too bright, tone them down by adding a little black or brown paint.

If you are buying new paint the latest water-based wood stains for garden use are very good for timber containers. They protect the wood while still allowing the grain to show through and are harmless to plants.

The heart and the tulip were among the most common decorative patterns the settlers used, but other motifs, particularly those with religious connotations, were also popular. Stars, the sun, the moon, doves, lambs, cockerels, the cross and the crown were more than just decoration – each reminded the family of the importance of religion within their daily lives.

Simple designs can be hand-drawn or traced from a source book and made into stencils – buy oiled card from an art shop if you wish to use them more than once. If a pattern is a little crooked or smudged it really doesn't matter – it will add to the simple charm of your American Country container.

American Country style need not be solely inspired by the early settlers; regional and cultural variations mean that there is a wealth of possible sources for ideas and inspiration.

New England style is characterized by clapboard houses, picket fences, painted birdhouses and Adirondack chairs, and uses a lighter, brighter, palette with lots of white and shades of blue. Wooden tubs, planters and window boxes are less crudely made and are painted to complement the colour of the house in a much more considered way than in the gardens of the early settlers. Planting is an informal mixture of herbaceous perennials and cottage-garden annuals. A seaside garden, a clapboard house or even a wooden shed can be the setting for New England-style containers. Instead of tinware and old pots and pans, use enamelled pails, bowls and jugs as planters and decorative accessories, and erect picket fencing to define the area.

On the eastern seaboard it is inevitable that the style of gardening and many of the plants have their origins in Europe. The further south and west you move the more this influence fades, and the more important native plants become.

The earliest inhabitants, the Native Americans, gathered herbs and flowers from the wild for medicines and any plants which were cultivated were for food. Many of the flowers we grow were first used by the Native Americans for their medicinal properties, including bergamot (*Monarda didyma*), which we now consider a cottage-garden plant.

How you interpret American Country depends on your location. If you live somewhere hot and dry you would do better to emulate the gardens and container-planting of New Mexico and Arizona rather than trying to grow thirsty plants which will never thrive in the heat. There are wonderful, colourful American native plants which will be happy in these conditions, including salvias, dahlias, zinnias and cosmos. With walls painted in earth colours, plants can be grown in turquoise-painted tin cans as well as clay pots, and they can include cacti and succulents as well as bright flowers. This scheme would also work well in a modern south-facing conservatory in more temperate regions.

The hot, humid climate of the South is redolent of rampant vines and fragrant flowers. Here creepers scramble over porches painted in sugared-almond colours and pots overflow with tropical plants. Quick-growing annual climbers such as morning glory (*Ipomoea hederacea*), black-eyed Susan (*Thunbergia alata*) and the cup-and-saucer vine (*Cobaea scandens*) will provide suitably lush growth and exotic flowers, especially when teamed with climbing perennials and shrubs. Confederate jasmine (*Trachelospermum jasminoides*) is an evergreen climber with wonderfully scented panicles of flowers and the glossy green leaves of gardenia (*Gardenia augusta*) mean that this shrub is attractive even when it isn't in flower. Provided you are able to water them regularly, all these plants will do well in a sheltered south-facing position or in a conservatory. The gardenia will need frost protection in winter. If your climate is not humid the best way to provide optimum conditions for these plants when grown on a terrace or patio or in a conservatory is to water the floor in hot weather to create humidity.

Choosing the plants for your American Country containers has more to do with creating an illusion than with historical or geographical accuracy. Provided the overall look is right, only the most pernickety (and well-informed) visitor is going to point out any inaccuracies.

Tulips, however, are very appropriate plants for the American Country spring garden. In 16th-century Europe the bulb, newly imported from Asia Minor, caused a sensation and fortunes were made and lost speculating on crops of particularly prized varieties such as 'Semper Augustus', which could command a price of £1000 for a single bulb. Tulipomania, as it was known, guaranteed that this flower was universally known, and even after the market collapsed it still retained a mystique and romance which meant that settlers took their precious bulbs with them to cultivate in the New World. Tulips planted with other spring flowers such as muscari, forget-me-nots, anemones and bellis daisies in containers painted with heart or tulip motifs make a style of garden that would be familiar to the Pennsylvania Dutch gardener.

Recommended tulip varieties for a cottage-garden look include 'Angélique', a paeony-flowered pink tulip, *Tulipa greigii*, with maroon and purple veining on the leaves, and *T*. 'Red Riding Hood', which has fiery red flowers. Taller-stemmed varieties will need some support and this can be provided by

inserting rustic twigs around the perimeter of the pot and winding string around to create a supporting frame. This is both practical and decorative.

Planted baskets will eventually weather and perish, but you can prolong their life by coating the basket with an outdoor varnish or alternatively lining the base and sides with black polythene before planting – punch some drainage holes in the plastic first to allow any excess water to drain away.

Containers are very versatile and with new decoration, another position or different plants you can ring the changes without having to buy or make any new containers. When the spring display is over you can either choose plants within the same colour range for your summer display, or go for a complete change of scene with entirely different colours. Keep in mind that the essence of American Country is simple containers and informal planting and you won't go far wrong.

If you want to include a selection of native American plants in your containers there are plenty of varieties which should be easy to obtain wherever you live. The flowering tobacco, *Nicotiana*, has its origins in the New World. Choose the taller-growing white tobacco *N. alata* if you want the evening-scented variety, as the bedding varieties, although more compact and available in a variety of colours, do not have the same fragrance. Another plant with a delicious evening fragrance is evening primrose (*Oenothera missouriensis*). *Phlox divaricata* susbp. *laphamii* 'Chattahoochee' is a wonderful summer container plant with clouds of long-lasting soft blue flowers. The smaller varieties of penstemons grow happily in a mixed planting, flowering from midsummer right through to the autumn, and the cone flower (*Echinacea purpurea*), with its magenta-petalled flowers, is a decorative plant in a large container.

Seaside

The seashore is a rich source of materials and inspiration for container planting. Driftwood, shells, weathered rope and sea-smoothed pebbles can all be used as decorations on or around pots planted with easy-to-grow maritime plants, which include grasses, succulents and silver-leaved plants.

I N H I G H S U M M E R there is no better place to be than at the seaside. Nearly all of us have happy memories of idyllic childhood holidays spent paddling in rock pools, building sandcastles and beachcombing and we return to the seashore as adults to recapture that experience with our own children. For those of us lucky enough to live by the sea, any sunny day is a temptation to wander down to the beach and see what the tide has brought in.

We associate the seaside with holidays and relaxation, and the use of a maritime theme in the garden can create a haven of calm whatever the garden's location – there is no need to actually live near the sea to be inspired by it. This is a style which draws its source from the old-fashioned seaside resorts of Scandinavia and Britain, the ports of Brittany and the Côte Atlantique and the seaboards of North America. The keyword is simplicity, with pale blue and white being the predominant colours. Boardwalks and white-painted shiplap timber, wooden decking and shell-decorated galvanized buckets sit alongside sea-worn driftwood and weathered wooden barrels with nautical rope handles.

Plants are chosen for their resilience, as they must thrive in bracing sea breezes, and for their cool shades of blue, grey and lilac. Grasses, sea hollies (*Eryngium*), scabious (*Scabiosa*), sea lavender (*Limonium*), santolina, juniper and thrift (*Armeria maritima*) are hardy, easy-going plants which are ideal for dry, sunny gardens, or where regular attention is not always possible. These planting schemes also fit well into gravel gardens or those where there is a predominance of pebbles, cobbles or stone. If you choose drought-loving plants which positively thrive on little water the containers can be left unattended for a week or two without coming to any harm. It is a good idea to include a high proportion of silver-leaved plants and grasses, as they will have a long season of interest and can look as good in autumn and spring as they do in high summer. Good drainage is essential for most of these plants, so it is vital that they are planted in free-draining soil in containers which do not retain water.

LEFT: *A pot planted with* Festuca glauca *is garlanded with a rope of sea shells.*

RIGHT: *In a seashore garden a weathered boat shelters pots of ornamental grasses and lavender.*

Craft Project 3

SEASIDE WINDOW BOX

THIS WINDOW BOX is made from 15mm (⅝in) thick recycled wood with a rough-hewn finish. The rope handles at each end are both appropriate to the seaside theme and make the window box very easy to move.

Construction

1. Using a hand or electric saw cut the front, back, and two side panels to the dimensions given.

2. Draw box joints 25mm (1in) wide at both ends of the front and back panels. Make the depth the same as the timber thickness, or 25mm (1in) deep for more decorative corners. Draw opposing joints at both ends of the side panels. Roughly cut out the joints with the jigsaw and tidy with chisel.

3. Test that the joints fit snugly, then apply glue to all meeting surfaces and join the front, back and sides. Nail together at each top corner.

4. Turn the box upside down and carefully measure the base. Cut a baseboard to fit, glue and nail it in place, and drill drainage holes.

5. Drill holes for rope handles halfway down each side panel, with each hole 50mm (2in) from the centre. Cut the rope in half, thread each half through the holes and knot the ends inside. Paint the box with off-white wood stain.

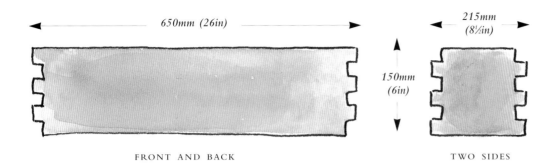

650mm (26in)

215mm
(8½in)

150mm
(6in)

FRONT AND BACK

TWO SIDES

1. Cut front, back and side panels to dimensions given and cut out interlocking box joints using a jigsaw..

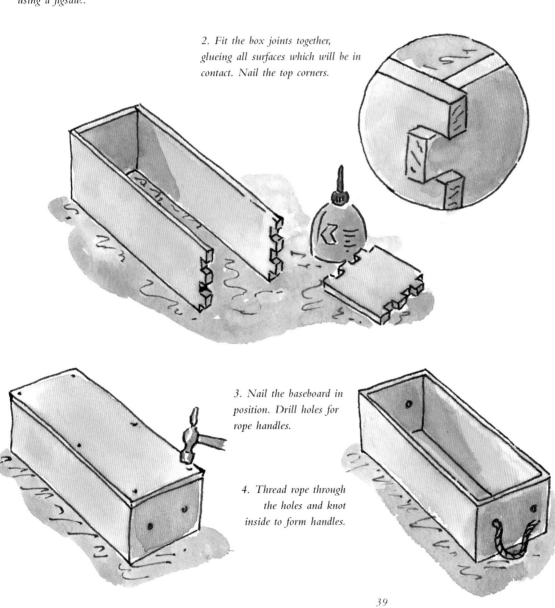

2. Fit the box joints together, glueing all surfaces which will be in contact. Nail the top corners.

3. Nail the baseboard in position. Drill holes for rope handles.

4. Thread rope through the holes and knot inside to form handles.

GRASSES, RUSHES & SEDGES

After years of neglect, grasses have now become popular garden plants with a strong following. Their splendid architectural outlines and wide range of leaf-colour make them eye-catching container plants that thrive on neglect.

In their hurry to fill containers with colourful flowers, gardeners often forget that as much pleasure can be derived from plants with a simpler appearance. Grasses and other foliage plants have the potential to be more elegant, more understated and more restful to the eye than traditional shrubs and flowers. In certain styles of garden, or in a particular area of a garden, they give exactly the right cool look. Leaf colours range from the palest greys and icy blues right through to the most vibrant greens and even red, but it is the slim leaf shapes that characterize this group of plants. Grasses do flower, some more flamboyantly than

Miscanthus sinensis 'Morning Light'

Miscanthus sinensis 'Gracillinus'

others, and the flowerheads tend to be slender, delicate panicles, thrown up in spires above the foliage. Left untrimmed they will create a soft halo above the plant throughout the winter and will look marvellously ethereal when hung with dewdrops or rimed with frost.

Technically speaking, grasses, rushes and sedges have different botanical characteristics, but from the gardener's point of view they can be grouped together and called 'grasses'. Most grasses which have an arching or clump-forming habit can be grown in containers, although it is best to exclude those which like damp soil such as

Helictotrichon sempervirens

Schoenoplectus lacustris and the *Typha* species, which are really water plants and happiest on the margins of a pond.

VARIEGATED GRASSES

An excellent and reliable variegated grass is *Hakonechloa macra* 'Aureola', which forms a symmetrical mound about 20–25cm (8–10 in) tall and 40cm (16in) across. The green leaves are striped with gold and take on a reddish hue towards the autumn, when similarly toned flower stalks may appear. To look its best this grass needs a cool spot in shade or semi-shade and should be kept moist. Cat owners should note

that felines will find this plant quite irresistible and will eat it in preference to any other grass, so it should be positioned on a narrow ledge or in some other spot where they will find it hard to chew on its leaves!

Carex siderosticha 'Variegata' is a variegated sedge, with green leaves edged with cream. It produces its slender flower spikes in the spring. The height is around 30cm (12in) and the spread about 40cm (16in). It prefers to grow in a semi-shaded position. *Carex oshimensis* 'Evergold' is a more compact sedge with yellow-striped leaves and insignificant flower spikes.

Stipa calamagrostis

BLUE GRASSES

For blue colours the *Festuca* group, known as fescues or blue grasses, have the best colour range. They are generally small, rarely reaching over 30cm (12in) in height, and have a fine, almost ephemeral appearance. Fescues like a well-drained soil in full sun and can stand a reasonable amount of drought, so container-growing should present no problems. All the forms of *F. glauca* have a good blue colour and some, like the 10cm (4in) *F. g.* 'Minima', are perfect for alpine pans or tiny pots. *Koeleria glauca* is a similar but more substantial grass. Low, dense mounds of intensely blue-grey leaves are topped by upright flowerheads of the same colour. It reaches a height of 20cm (8in). The slightly larger *K. macrantha* 'Silver Sea' (also known as 'Silbersee') is the bluest of all, appearing powder blue when grown in full sun. Still in the blue-grey spectrum but on a larger scale is *Helictotrichon sempervirens*, a hardy evergreen grass which

Hakonechloa macra

Growing Grasses

In general grasses are tolerant of hot, dry conditions, but check the label before buying in case the plant you have chosen is an exception. Provided the plant is suitable for dry conditions pot it into a soil-based compost such as John Innes No. 2, to which 25 per cent coarse grit has been added to ensure very free drainage. Cover the surface of the soil around the plant with further coarse grit or, better still, smooth pebbles, which are more in keeping with the seaside theme. In early spring cut back the old foliage as new growth begins.

Hakonechloa macra 'Aureola'

forms an attractively dense clump about 60cm (2ft) across. This grass grows naturally on the stony hillsides of the European Alps, so for best results give it a sunny position and make sure the compost is free-draining.

ARCHITECTURAL GRASSES

With large containers such as half barrels or old tin baths gardeners can experiment with some of the bolder forms of grasses. *Miscanthus sinensis* is one of the most widely grown, generally reaching around 1.8m (6ft) high, with feathery flower plumes which appear in late summer and give subtle colour throughout the winter. Two more compact forms are *M. s.* 'Gracillimus', which grows to a height of 1.5m (5ft), and *M. s.* 'Morning Light', which has very delicate striped foliage.

Some of the prettiest flowerheads are to be found in the *Stipa* group, which throw up arching feathery panicles that wave gracefully in the breeze. *S. calamagrostis* is longlasting in flower, bearing its greenish-white panicles from summer to late autumn, but at 75cm (2½ft) across and 1.2m (4ft) high it will need a substantial container. *S. tenuissima* is more delicate, with narrow leaves and light, airy flowerheads and an overall height of about 60cm (2ft). Stipas like to be grown in the sun and will need a good rich compost and regular watering.

There are certain elements that will help you establish the seaside theme in your garden. As with American Country style, you can transform the most unpromising outhouse or shed into an appropriate backdrop for your containers. A wooden garden shed need be no less functional because it has been painted white with forget-me-not blue trim and has a faded beach-hut curtain hanging just inside the door. A black-stained, weather-boarded outhouse with a sunshine-yellow door and windowframe may in reality contain bikes and the garden furniture, but it can also be a perfect setting for a pebble and wildflower garden inspired by that of the late film-maker Derek Jarman.

In many old fishing ports the houses are packed closely together and what gardens there are consist of little courtyards and narrow alleyways. The walls are painted white and plants are crammed into all sorts of unlikely containers from large seashells to coils of oiled rope. You can give your city backyard a similar treatment or even brighten a dark alleyway. In cool, damp areas it may not be possible to grow sun-loving plants, but there are grasses such as *Miscanthus* and *Hakonechloa* which like such conditions. If they are planted in pots topped with smooth pebbles and accompanied by an old anchor propped against the wall with some driftwood hung above it, a previously unpromising paved yard lacks

ABOVE: *Sea campion (*Silene uniflora*) and a variegated* Arabis *form a tabletop still life.*

RIGHT: *Weathered terracotta pots hold ornamental grasses surrounded by a mulch of sea shells.*

only the distant sound of the sea and the cry of the gulls.

Seashells are fashionable decorative accessories, so even if you live nowhere near the sea you will have little problem getting hold of some. Your local department store is likely to sell net bags of spotlessly clean shells to use as bathroom decorations – they may look a bit too pristine, but a few weeks out in the garden will soon fix that. If you have collected your shells yourself you should bear in mind their fishy origins – in a confined space, and especially under cover in a porch or conservatory, they can smell awful in hot weather. Boil them for at least an hour to remove any debris and then leave them

to soak in a bowl of cold water to which you have added a small quantity of bleach or disinfectant – they may no longer smell of the sea, but neither will they smell of something a lot less pleasant. When using shells as

decoration try not to overdo things; a few seashells look stylish, seashells everywhere tend to look rather tacky.

People who live by the sea don't tend to go in for fancy paintwork, decorative patterns or stencils on the outside of their houses – any decoration is fairly straightforward and designed to withstand winter gales and lashing rain. Weathering by the elements is an inadvertent paint effect which many wish they could avoid, but which undoubtedly adds charm to the scene. Resist the temptation to paint all your seaside pots, barrels and window boxes freshly every year- a couple of years of weathering will give them an authentically distressed look.

One of the great pleasures of choosing a seaside theme for your containers is that it gives you an excuse to visit a beach and scour the shore for interesting bits and pieces. A walk along the shoreline becomes a voyage of discovery as well as good exercise. Take a plastic bag with you, as it's very frustrating to leave behind choice pickings because your pockets are crammed.

Aficionados of the art of beachcombing will tell you that the best finds follow stormy weather when the whole shoreline has been rearranged and new treasures are revealed. This is when you are most likely to find unusual shells and particularly fine pieces of driftwood in among the detritus of modern life.

When you are shell-collecting, don't disregard the common seashells. Mussel shells with their blue-black sheen look great as a decorative mulch in the top of a pot, particularly when wet, or they can be used like mosaic tiles to decorate an entire pot or just edge the rim. Similarly, scallop shells have a beautiful symmetry about them that makes them a perfect decorative device; use them to decorate pots, or arrange a row of them to outline a doorway or a windowframe. You don't need to visit a beach to obtain mussel or scallop shells – you can save them from a seafood meal or ask your local fishmonger for shells he would otherwise throw away. However you collect them, clean them as described on page 42 or you will find

MAIN PICTURE, LEFT: *Sea thrift (Armeria maritima) and* Artemisia *are good choices for a seaside window box as they will withstand buffeting winds and salt spray.*

ABOVE: *Succulents and silver-leaved plants such as crassula and rosemary grow well in a seaside garden.*

your garden will be too authentically fishy for most people's taste!

If you are lucky you may pick up lengths of rope along the shore, but you will need to be quick off the mark – no-one can resist an abandoned length of rope. Use it to coil round and conceal a large plastic pot or simply let it coil among a group of pots.

Although you will be able to obtain shells and rope elsewhere, you really do need to visit the beach for authentic pieces of driftwood. Large pieces require a certain amount of muscle and determination, but can be well worth the effort. With their weathered, sculptured qualities they need no embellishment to make a focal point among your seaside containers. A piece with one relatively flat surface can be used to make a shelf on which to display pots of grasses or succulents or decorative bits and pieces. Driftwood does not have to be large to be usable – small pieces mixed with smooth pebbles and small seashells make an excellent and attractive mulch to use in the top of pots around your plants, but bear in mind that if your plants aren't salt-tolerant your mulch ingredients will need a long soak in fresh water before use. Driftwood frames are very popular, and you can make your own using a cheap flat-faced frame as your base and gluing or tacking the pieces of driftwood in place. Use it to outline a wallpot containing a colourful flowering succulent such as a *Lampranthus* or *Portulaca*.

If you live at some distance from the coast you will have to confine beachcombing to holidays, but you should still be able to find suitable containers and decorative pieces by scouring your local junk shops and going to car boot or garage sales. After a few years most people clear out mementos of seaside visits and these sales can provide rich pickings.

Look out for battered galvanized pails and baths to use as planters. Blue enamelware is also very much in keeping with the seaside theme and because few people want a jug or bucket which is badly chipped or has a hole in it you should be able to pick them up for next to nothing.

Seaside is not just one style – there are many beach houses which incorporate every possible interpretation with bright beach hut stripes, ropes and anchors, shells and fishing nets all jumbled together in a glorious muddle.

This can work well set against the backdrop of a working harbour but looks quite ludicrous in other locations. Choose your favourite interpretation and stick to it. If the cool, rather Scandinavian colours used in this chapter seem too subdued to you, go for brighter blues set off by bright whites and introduce yellows and oranges to your planting. *Gazania*, *Osteospermum*, *Kniphofia* (red-hot poker), *Eschscholzia* (California poppy) and

OPPOSITE: *In a sheltered spot a winter hanging basket will remain colourful well into the new year.*

RIGHT: *An old enamel basin makes an excellent container for* Hakonechloa macra *'Aureola',* Osteospermum *'Buttermilk' and* Eschscholzia.

Lampranthus are all plants with a good range of yellows and oranges that will do well in coastal gardens or inland.

A more dramatic statement can be made with a strongly coloured background such as the black and sunshine yellow used by the late Derek Jarman to paint his beach house in his Dungeness garden. Around the house stones, driftwood and pieces of rusted metal have been arranged to emphasize their sculptural qualities and indigenous plants such as *Eryngium maritimum* (sea holly), *Glaucium flavum* (horned poppy), *Limonium* (sea lavender) and *Crambe maritima* (sea kale) seed themselves to create an extraordinary display. Although some of these plants would not grow well in containers or away from the coast, there are related plants with similar architectural qualities that could be substituted – for instance, *Eryngium giganteum* instead of *E. maritimum, Crambe cordifolia* instead of *C. maritima* and an ordinary lavender instead of sea lavender. In the spirit of this style of gardening, use old black enamel cooking pots, rusty buckets and corrugated iron tubs as containers or conceal the containers altogether under drifts of shingle or smooth stones. This sort of planting would look great in a contemporary architectural setting.

47

Choosing the plants for your seaside containers depends very much on your location and climate. An exposed coastal position would be ideally suited to the grasses, succulents and shoreline plants which have been featured in this chapter, while a sheltered courtyard near the coast or in an urban setting could grow more tender plants such as *Agave*, *Aeonium*, *Yucca* and *Agapanthus*, along with hardy palms such as the Chusan palm (*Trachycarpus fortunei*) and plants with striking architectural leaves such as *Fatsia japonica* and phormiums. All of these plants are quite exotic in appearance and they will give the garden a sub-tropical flavour. Given the right conditions, they will grow very large. They will need regular feeding during the growing season and will probably need to be repotted every other year.

Large wooden tubs or half barrels make ideal final containers for the larger plants. Before planting them up it is a good idea to drill holes near the top of the tub or barrel and attach rope handles, as this will make it easier if you need to move them in the future. Use a soil mixture which consists of at least 50 per cent enriched loam such as John Innes No. 3 added to a standard potting

LEFT: *A shell-encrusted pot is planted with a variegated* Agapanthus *and the delicate grass* Nassella trichotoma.

ABOVE: *A stone with a hole in it makes an unusual and attractive home for a small succulent.*

compost and add extra coarse grit to ensure good drainage.

Although there are exceptions, most maritime plants like to grow in a very free-draining soil, and once established they do not need a great deal of water. However, it is always true that container plants require more water than those that are grown directly in the soil. Shoreline plants that appear to be growing in nothing more than stones or shingle will often send roots way down in search of water, but container plants do not have this resource. While maritime plants may like to have access to water they definitely do not like to stand in it, so rather than providing each pot with a saucer, which can create quite humid conditions, you will do better to spread a thick layer of shingle or gravel under the pots. Not only will this benefit the plants, it will also contribute to the seaside theme.

There are many plants which do very well in hot, dry conditions and are also tolerant of salt-laden breezes, although

they will do best if not too exposed to strong winds; in coastal gardens they will need to be protected from the prevailing winds by a wall or fence. Members of the *Cistus* genus make handsome shrubs which flower for several weeks in the summer. *C. purpureus* is easy to grow and hardy, and has purplish-pink flowers blotched with deep red on each petal. *C. × corbariensis* is another easy cistus, with white flowers. *Phygelius × rectus*, with its yellow, orange or terracotta-coloured flowers, is another handsome shrub which adapts well to a container, although it will need dividing after three years to keep it flowering well. In cooler gardens it tends to lose its foliage over winter, in which case it should be left untrimmed until spring when all the old growth should be removed as new shoots appear.

All the silver- and grey-leaved herbs will do well in a dry garden, including *Santolina*, *Artemisia*, *Helichrysum italicum* (curry plant), sage, *Phlomis fruticosa* (Jerusalem sage), rosemary and rue, as will other silver-leaved plants such as *Stachys lanata*, *Verbascum*, *Senecio*, *Convolvulus cneorum* and *Anthemis punctata* subsp. *cupaniana*. Grow them in a loam-based compost to which coarse grit has been added and if they have been grown on in a peat-based compost be sure to soak them well before transplanting and gently loosen the rootball. Top with a decorative mulch of grit, pebbles or seashells.

Decorated Country

Inspired by the decorative traditions

of many countries, Decorated Country

uses painted patterns to transform simple

containers into something special. Bright

and beautiful plants are used to

emphasize each of the decorative themes.

Each of the projects requires only

basic painting skills.

I N THIS CHAPTER traditional folk art patterns from around the world are given a modern interpretation, with bold use of colour and design. All of us have a history of decorative patterns in our lives, based on regional traditions or family history. In the past, if you lived in Scandinavia you would have decorated your home, inside and outside, with local folk art patterns; if your family then emigrated to America you would have taken those traditional patterns with you and slowly those same patterns would have been assimilated and adapted by a wider populace. American Country (see pages 22–35) is an example of how the blending of traditional decorative styles from all over Europe resulted in something totally new and uniquely American.

Folk art is always evolving in this way because it is the art of the people, not of the artistic elite. There are no rules, just traditional materials and patterns which are freely adapted depending on the skill and inclination of the individual. This is a chance for you to give free rein to your creativity without restraint. If you feel inspired to combine Indian patterns with a Scandinavian palette, give it a try – it may look fabulous. If

you haven't done this type of decorating before you may feel safer at first in copying one of the container ideas, but as you gain confidence you can start adding personal touches which will make your Decorated Country container uniquely yours.

Planting is similarly unrestrained by forms or conventions – in some instances colours are vivid and freely mixed, while others seek to echo the tones of the container with unusual flower or foliage colour. More than any other style in this book, this one allows experimentation and this includes the choice of plants. Not long ago there was a fashion for using only the subtlest of colours in the garden but gradually this has changed, thanks to the influence of innovative gardeners such as Christopher Lloyd at Great Dixter. The fun has been brought back to gardening with glorious displays of intensely colourful flowers guaranteed to brighten the dullest of surroundings.

LEFT: *The delicate tracery on the fernwork pots is complemented by the foliage and flowers of a white aquilegia, Viola 'Irish Molly' and variegated foliage.*

RIGHT: *A bold tabletop display uses fernwork pots planted with* Heuchera *'Chocolate Ruffles' and a bright green ornamental grass.*

Craft Project 4

FERNWORK POTS

YOU WILL NEED
- An unglazed terracotta pot, preferably with a rough finish
- A selection of fresh fern fronds
- A newspaper
- Books to use as weights
- A protective face mask

TERRACOTTA POTS are used for a modern interpretation of the old craft of fernwork popular in Victorian England. Wooden pieces such as trays, letter racks and picture frames were first grained and varnished and then stencilled in black using pressed fern fronds as templates.

Construction

1. Spread the fern fronds between layers of newspaper, ensuring they are not bent as this might spoil the silhouette. Place heavy books on top of the newspaper and leave overnight or longer.

2. Carefully remove the ferns from between the layers of newspaper and spray the front of each with a coating of aerosol glue.

3. Apply the ferns to the pots. As the ferns are delicate you will need to position them correctly first time as you won't be able to readjust them without tearing.

4. Take the pot outside, put on the face mask and lightly and smoothly spray the pot with the black paint from a distance of about 20cm (8in). It is better to apply two very light coats of paint rather than one heavy one as this will tend to form drips.

5. Leave to dry completely, then carefully peel away the fern leaves to reveal the fernwork pattern.

TO DECORATE
- Aerosol mounting spray
- Matt black aerosol paint

1. *Spread fern leaves between layers of newspaper and press with heavy books.*

2. *Spray leaves with aerosol glue and mount on pot.*

3. *In a well-ventilated space, spray paint the pot.*

4. *When the paint is dry, carefully peel off the leaves.*

Adapting a Good Idea

With their many fronds, fern leaves are an ideal shape for silhouette decoration, but you can also press other leaves and flowers for this kind of decorative finish provided you can achieve a crisp outline.

Black on brown is the traditional colouring for fernwork, but you can give it an entirely new look by using different colours. Spray the pot gold, mount the ferns and then spray again with silver paint and you will have a pattern of gold ferns on a silver background.

Faking Age

Freshly decorated, these pots would look wonderful in a contemporary setting. For more traditional surroundings, gently rub over the pattern with fine sandpaper to allow some of the terracotta to show through the black paint.

FLOWER POWER

*Abandon restraint and go for vibrantly colourful plants for
your containers. You will find that even so-called 'clashing'
colours that would make you wince elsewhere will
combine happily in the garden.*

Rudbeckia hirta 'Marmalade'

It is such a relief to return to bright colours after all those years of restrained planting and discover that colourful does not have to mean vulgar. Petunias, zinnias, alyssum, phlox and nasturtium have long been country-garden favourites with their kaleidoscopic colours and it's wonderful to have them back brightening our borders and tumbling out of containers. Many colourful plants are annuals grown from seed each year or bought as young plants from the garden centres, or half-hardy perennials such as pelargoniums,

dahlias and fuchsias, which can be overwintered or discarded at the end of the season.

STRONG YELLOWS

Plant with oranges and greens for harmony or purple for contrast. For large containers it's hard to beat the sunflower, which is now available in multi-headed dwarf varieties (a relative term) for container-growing. Other recommended tall plants are the yellow-flowered *Abutilon* 'Canary Bird', dahlias in yellow shades, *Argyranthemum* 'Jamaica Primrose' or 'Maderense', all of which are half-hardy and perennials, and *Rudbeckia hirta* 'Marmalade' or

Eschscholzia californica

'Goldilocks' and *Coreopsis* 'Sunray', all of which can be grown as annuals. For smaller containers look out for yellow varieties of *Zinnia, Nemesia, Viola, Calendula* and *Antirrhinum*, as well as the poached-egg plant *Limnanthes douglasii*. The trailing *Bidens ferulifolia* is excellent for large hanging baskets and *Lysimachia nummularia* 'Aurea' has bright yellow-green trailing foliage.

INTENSE ORANGES

Plant with yellow and bright red for harmony or bright blue for contrast. A large tub or barrel looks wonderful planted with the Mexican sunflower *Tithonia*

Dahlia 'Bishop of Llandaff'

Salvia patens

rotundifolia 'Torch'. For a really stunning display, plant it with *Verbena bonariensis*. The tall-flowering stems of the verbena will grow through the tithonia so that by midsummer a cloud of purple flowers will be hovering above the orange tithonia flowers. Black-eyed Susan (*Thunbergia alata*) is an excellent annual climber with showy orange flowers. The tiger lily (*Lilium tigrinum*) grows strongly in containers and looks particularly wonderful surrounded with bronze fennel. *Zinnia, Calendula, Mimulus, Eschscholzia* (Californian poppy) and *Tropaeolum* (nasturtium) with their vivid orange flowers will all do well in small containers.

ROBUST REDS

Plant with orange and purple for harmony and bright turquoise for contrast. The pelargonium is the star-performing red flower, unrivalled in the intensity of its colouring and undemanding nature. For tall growth *Geum* 'Mrs J. Bradshaw' is wonderful scrambling through other plants, especially *Dahlia* 'Bishop of Llandaff' with its dark red foliage and vermilion flowers or *Fuchsia* 'Thalia' with red-tubular flowers and bronze foliage. The pineapple sage (*Salvia elegans*) is a wonderfully fragrant shrub with bright scarlet flowers, ideal for a container. *Tropaeolum majus* 'Empress of India' has intensely red flowers and is ideal for a container or hanging basket, as is *Verbena* 'Lawrence Johnston'.

PULSATING PINKS

Plant with warm reds and purples for harmony and lime green for contrast. Cerise pelargoniums can be so intensely colourful that they hurt the eye but they can be cooled down by planting with feathery-leaved *Cosmos*. *Verbena* 'Sissinghurst' is a reliable favourite with shocking pink flowers which trail from hanging baskets or tumble over the sides of containers all summer. It combines well with shocking pink petunias and for a really intense burst of colour you could include *Salvia*

Verbena 'Homestead Purple'

buchananii, with glossy green leaves and Schiaparelli pink furry flowers.

VELVETY PURPLES

Plant with warm reds and blues for harmony and bright yellows for contrast. *Verbena bonariensis* has long stems bearing sprays of purple flowers well above other flowers, while the lower-growing *V.* 'Homestead Purple' is perfect for smaller containers. *Fuchsia* 'Winston Churchill' has striking

Verbena 'Sissinghurst'

purple and cerise flowers and *Penstemon* 'Papal Purple' is a perennial which will do well in a pot, but the most intense purples of the summer can be found in the flowers of heliotrope and petunias. The purple-leaved sage *Salvia purpurea* has purple-red foliage early in the summer, but this tends to fade as the season progresses, while *Heuchera micrantha* var. *diversifolia* 'Palace Purple' is more wine than purple. Whether you

Alchemilla mollis

include lavender depends on whether you consider its flowers to be purple or blue – or lavender!

BRILLIANT BLUES

Plant with purple and turquoise for harmony and orange for contrast. A pot of morning glory *Ipomoea* 'Heavenly Blue' is guaranteed to delight you as it greets you daily with its newly opened flowers. Grow in peat pots in order to avoid root disturbance when transplanting. *Salvia patens* can be kept from year to year if it is dried off like a dahlia tuber at the end of the season. Its intensely blue flowers are worth the effort. *Cerinthe major* is an unusual plant with blue-green bracts which positively glow with colour at twilight. Deep blue varieties of *Lobelia*, *Felicia*, *Brachyscome* and the fan-flower *Scaevola* are all reliable container plants which can also be used in hanging baskets.

LUSCIOUS LIMES

Plant with yellows and greens for harmony and cerise pink for contrast. Although there aren't that many lime green flowers, those there are can be very useful in the garden. *Alchemilla mollis* is an easy-to-grow perennial which will thrive in a pot and its delicate lime green flowers combine wonderfully with sweet peas. Lime-green *Nicotiana affinis* and *N. langsdorffii* will do best in a large container in partial shade, while *Zinnia* 'Envy' prefers a hot, sunny spot.

To use colour really well in the garden, or anywhere else for that matter, it is useful to know a little about basic colour theory. This is based on a circle divided into 12 segments which progress through the colours of the spectrum from pure red through oranges, yellows, greens, blues, purples, violets and back to red – just like the rainbow but with extra gradations of colour. Colours that adjoin one another, for example red, yellow and orange, are 'harmonious' and will always blend well together. Most of us instinctively aim for harmony in our garden, which is why garden centres now sell colour-themed packs of plants.

Colours that are directly opposite one another in the colour circle are known as 'complementary' and will intensify one another. This is why orange pansies planted with royal blue lobelia positively throb with colour or lime green nicotiana combined with cerise pelargoniums make such impact. This certainly doesn't mean that everything in the garden should be planted with its complementary colour – indeed it would be visually exhausting – but the occasional splash of a complementary colour can add vitality to your planting. For example, a group of pots planted with a selection of purple heliotrope, petunias and verbena will draw the eye much more effectively if a yellow *Bidens ferulifolia* trails among the other flowers.

Like all good rules, the rules of colour are guidelines only, and are often most useful when helping you sort out why something doesn't work, rather than providing a rigid framework within which you should work. Because colours seldom clash in nature it can be exciting to experiment with 'off' colours which might jar in other circumstances such as orange and pink or purple and turquoise. There is a visual excitement inherent in daring combinations which can give your containers real drama. Interestingly, the one plant colour that can cause problems is white – when combined with strongly coloured flowers, white plants cheapen the effect. Confine

white plants to pastel planting or use them very sparingly.

Folk artists often have an intuitive understanding of colour, which they apply with great exuberance to anything they decorate. The hot colours of Indian fabrics, the vibrant hues of Mexican pottery, the cooler, softer tones of Scandinavian folk art – each palette reflects the local colours seen in the neighbouring natural world which are then carried through into decorative art.

Taking our inspiration from these traditions, we can use colour in the same way to enhance pots, tubs and planters and even experiment with coloured backgrounds against which plants can be seen at their best. The starting point is often the most basic of containers – a plain terracotta pot, a simple wooden trough, a collection of old tin cans; each can be transformed by imaginative decoration and good planting. Paint manufacturers are well aware of the renewed interest in a brighter palette, and just as they are producing 'historic colours' which allow us to faithfully reproduce traditional colour schemes, so they are also producing ranges of paints which encompass the 'spice' colours of India and the 'sherbet' colours of the Caribbean.

Decorated Country takes traditional decorative effects from around the world and gives them a modern look. Home furnishing and interior style shops have been doing this commercially for some time. If you visit one of these stores it is worth taking a bit of extra time to look at their garden merchandise to see how they put things together and create a certain feel – there is nothing wrong in learning from the experts. You can find inspiration everywhere. When you watch travel programmes, for example, don't just watch the presenter, look at

the background and make a note of the colours used to paint houses, which plants are growing and what the containers are like. Glossy magazines often do their fashion photo shoots in exotic locations. Look at the props which have been used, as the stylists will have searched out the best the locality has to offer and are expert at evoking the atmosphere of a place with a few artfully placed decorative bits and pieces.

Your inspiration for Decorated Country need not be so far afield – you can find plenty to inspire you by visiting local gardens, both small and grand. Many private gardens are open in aid of charity and the owners will usually be more than happy to discuss their ideas with you. Take a notebook and a camera with you – you may think you will remember a successful plant grouping or an interesting paint effect, but as often as not some element will escape you when you try to recall it. Much that you see will be traditional, but it can be updated by using different colours and plants.

The Fernwork Pots project (see page 52) is a good example of how this can be done. In this case the colours are similar to those used originally, but nothing else is. Historically, fernwork was used inside the home to decorate wooden furniture. By adapting this idea for outside use it immediately gains a freshness and originality. This is further emphasized by using contemporary,

quite sculptural pots, instead of those of a traditional style. There is nothing old-fashioned in the result, especially once the pots are filled with plants which complement the design. A chimney-pot decorated with fernwork patterns would make a stunning plinth, especially if topped with a black urn-shaped pot holding an architectural plant such as *Melianthus major*. Three of the elements of this idea are very traditional – the chimney-pot, the fernwork pattern and the urn – but combining them in this way is a totally modern approach.

If the palette and style of traditional Scandinavian design appeal to you, you can do no better than to look to the books of Carl Larsson for inspiration. Like the English Pre-Raphaelites, Larsson took traditional designs, reinterpreted them and used them to great decorative effect inside and outside his home. You can follow his example by taking his designs and adapting them for use on your country containers. Bows, hearts and checks are favourite decorative motifs and by using paint in shades of blue and green and plants like marguerites, violas and pansies you can re-create some of the simple beauty of this style.

LEFT: *A miniature blue campanula is displayed to advantage in a powder-blue pot decorated with a stencilled lace pattern.*

RIGHT: *Lily-of-the-valley (Convallaria majalis) nestled in moss looks charming in a wooden window box painted with a pretty bow.*

W hen you have taken time and trouble to decorate containers it is important that their setting complements the design. Dramatic effects can be totally lost among pretty planting, and delicate designs can be overwhelmed when surrounded by strong colours. If Decorated Country appeals to you as a style you will need to consider the whole garden and not just the containers, rather as you would consider the whole room when introducing a new piece of furniture. This doesn't mean that every time you decorate a pot you will have to redesign your garden, but it does mean that it will be more successful if you keep the larger picture in mind as you work.

In the same way that you need to take the location of your garden and the quality of light into account when adopting a Mediterranean-style garden, you should do the same for Decorated Country if it is inspired by exotic locations. The hot colours of India, which look fabulous against an ultramarine sky and sub-tropical foliage, can look absurdly inappropriate in an English cottage garden. If, however, you quieten the colours slightly they will lose their luminosity and fit happily into the landscape. Paisley-patterned pots decorated in relatively soft shades will give an effect that is extremely colourful and reminiscent of the East without being overpowering. The paisley pattern itself, although originating in

LEFT: *Brightly painted pots decorated with traditional patterns and planted with vibrant flowers give the garden an Indian flavour.*

RIGHT: *A waterproof marker has been used to draw the paisley patterns on this pot.*

India, has been part of Western culture for hundreds of years and its use as a decorative device will fit in well anywhere. If you like the Indian patterns but are not terribly keen on bright hues, you could use colours based on earth pigments instead – shades of umber, sienna and ochre are the colours of spices and would make an excellent background for the paisley designs. Planted with bamboos, hostas, ornamental grasses and *Ligularia,* this would make an exotic-looking foliage garden which would do well in a shady spot.

Sometimes all that is needed to establish the theme is a particular colour of paint and a style of planting. For instance, you may like the idea of a Chinese inspired container garden. This can be achieved by using lacquer-red paint, maybe on background fence panels, or on a wooden bench (ideally Chinese Chippendale style). Plant evergreen shrubs, azaleas and lilies in glazed pots and hang out paper lanterns when your friends come to visit and the illusion will be complete. This is one instance where you really shouldn't need to decorate your own containers – Chinese pots are exported all over the world and are very inexpensive to purchase. For the country look choose

brown glazed pots – the painted porcelain pots will look much too sophisticated in this context.

If a Japanese garden is more to your liking, simple trellis panels made out of bamboo poles will completely change the appearance of an ordinary panelled fence, especially if the fence is first stained dark brown or black. Other elements typical of a Japanese garden are gravel, smooth river stones, moss and water, with the planting usually consisting of sculptural low-growing conifers, evergreens and ferns.

With climate changes causing reductions in rainfall in northern Europe more of us are getting used to gardening in dry conditions, and we can draw on the native flora of many countries when we choose plants for this type of garden.

Many Antipodean plants are now proving quite tolerant of cooler climates, especially when they are planted in a sheltered south-facing garden. Eucalyptus, wattle, phormiums, cordyline, helichrysums, grasses and small-leaved hebes like *Hebe cupressoides* are all plants which will do well provided they are grown in free-draining soil. Eucalyptus and wattle tend to grow too large for most containers, but the rest will do well in pots. Ideally the pots should be rough, hand-formed shapes rather than machine-made. Accent the theme by painting at least one of the pots with Aboriginal-style decoration, which uses a limited earth-tone palette and patterns that are composed mainly of circles and dots.

In Africa, clay pots are used for cooking, carrying and storage. The pots are often fired directly in the embers of a large fire and this gives them a wonderful rough texture and a blackened appearance. To give an ordinary clay pot this type of finish, mix some coarse sand and a little black pigment with PVA glue and paint it onto the surface of the pot. Plant the

pots with aloes and succulents for your own little corner of Africa.

Both African and Australian folk art tend to rely largely on earth pigments, so if you crave something a bit more colourful in your garden you can look for your inspiration to the Caribbean and Mexico.

Caribbean style could be described as colourful colonial. The architecture has its origins in Europe, but its exuberant decoration is inspired by the brilliant colours of the indigenous flora and fauna and the *joie de vivre* of the inhabitants. Go the whole hog and turn your garden shed into a Bahamian beach house by adding a wooden verandah and a corrugated iron roof and painting it sherbet pinks and greens. For containers, hammer drainage holes in catering-size tin cans and paint them with gloss paint. Line them up along the verandah, planted with colourful quick-growing annual climbers like black-eyed Susan (*Thunbergia alata*), canary creeper (*Tropaeolum canariensis*), morning glory (*Ipomea purpurea*) and

nasturtium (*Tropaeolum majus*). For larger-scale planting, paint a rusty old wheelbarrow or tin bath and fill it with fragrant marvel of Peru (*Mirabilis jalapa*) with its multi-coloured flowers. Add a large tub planted with a hibiscus and the picture will be complete.

The dahlia, zinnia, cosmos and even the 'African' marigold are native to Mexico. Mexican style is vibrant and uninhibited, with paint colours so bright they are fluorescent. If you love putting pink, purple, orange and lime green together you are a natural for a Mexican garden, although in cooler climates it may be wise to limit the strongest colours to the plants – a fluorescent pink wall with lime green woodwork doesn't look nearly as appealing away from the old hacienda. Use simple hand-made terracotta pots as containers and plant yuccas, aloes and succulents as a backdrop to the bright colours.

For many of us these flowers are the flowers of our childhood, the ones our grandfather or grandmother helped us to plant in our first garden, and even when they were out of fashion they still held a place in our hearts. Now we can revel in using them in a new cosmopolitan style that refers back to their countries of origin.

ABOVE: *The rich orangey-pink of the Guernsey lily* (Nerine sarniensis) *makes an ideal plant for inclusion in the 'Decorated Country' garden.*

OPPOSITE: *A peeling fence is given Caribbean-style charm with trailing plants tumbling from painted tin cans.*

English Country

Pots, tubs and sinks planted with tumbling flowers and foliage have always been essential elements of English Country style. Although an idyllic country cottage is the perfect setting for this type of planting, it can look good in any location as its charm is universal.

THE ARCHETYPAL ENGLISH Country garden with its winding paths and overflowing borders is something many of us dream of re-creating. It is a style rooted in history and tradition; some of the plants have always grown in England, some were introduced by the Romans homesick for their native Italy, and many were imported by the monks for their monastery gardens, where they were grown for their healing properties. Shakespeare mentions flowers which remain cottage-garden favourites today and the 16th-century writer Thomas Tusser recommended pinks, marigolds, larkspur, love-in-a-mist, pansies, sweet rocket and wallflowers for pots and window boxes – all flowers we know today and all of which can be grown easily from seed.

English Country style is basically a matter of choosing old-fashioned, scented plants and putting them together in a relaxed and informal way. Fashion-conscious gardeners may consider it too undisciplined, but to many ordinary gardeners the world over, it is the type of garden which most attracts them. Each year at the Chelsea Flower Show in London

thousands of people gaze in wonder at the displays and those with a country-garden theme are always the favourites. But this is artifice, achieved at vast expense and effort, while the essence of true English Country gardening is innovation, making something out of nothing, growing plants cheaply and begging seeds and cuttings from neighbours and friends. This is cooperative rather than competitive gardening, and generosity with your own surplus plants will soon open a wellspring of reciprocal generosity among fellow gardeners. Plants which have long ceased to be grown commercially still circulate in the gardening fraternity.

The beauty of this style is that although it originated in the villages and thatched cottages of medieval England, it no longer belongs to any particular period, area, or type of house. The principles of cottage gardening are stunningly simple and can be followed wherever you live.

LEFT: Scilla siberica *is a miniature bulb which is ideal for container culture.*

RIGHT: *Grouped around a cottage window, spring bulbs overflow from an eclectic selection of containers in typical cottage-garden style.*

Craft Project 5

BROKEN CHINA MOSAIC POT

Anyone with an established garden will find that pieces of broken china appear when the soil is turned over. In the absence of this source, buy chipped china from junk shops.

Construction

1. Use tile cement to fasten strip tiles along each side of the corners of the pot, cutting them to fit. Leave to set firm.
2. Spread the broken china on a flat surface. Discard pieces which are not flat, or markedly thicker or thinner.
3. Spread a generous layer of tile cement on one face of the pot, using the comb supplied. Press pieces of china firmly into the cement, working systematically from top to bottom or vice versa. If you need smaller fragments, place some china into the carrier bag, fold it over and hit sharply with the hammer.
4. Leave the mosaic pattern to harden slightly then wipe away the excess cement with a damp sponge. When the cement has set fully, clean the surface of the china using the bathroom cleaner. Repeat with the other three surfaces.
5. Wearing rubber gloves, apply the grout to the mosaic with your fingers, filling any gaps between the pieces to create a smooth finish. Wipe away excess with a damp sponge. Leave until nearly set, then use a soft cloth to remove any grout from the surface of the china.

1. Use tile cement to attach the strip tiles to the pot corners and leave to set.

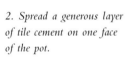

2. Spread a generous layer of tile cement on one face of the pot.

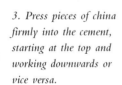

3. Press pieces of china firmly into the cement, starting at the top and working downwards or vice versa.

4. Leave the cement to harden slightly then wipe off excess with a damp sponge. When fully set, clean the surface with a bathroom cleaner, then grout to finish.

Alternative Materials

Broken china is not the only recycled material you can use for mosaics. Glass, smooth stones, bottle caps and sea shells all look effective.

A Round Mosaic Pot

To decorate a round pot in this style, use the strip tiles to divide the pot into vertical segments, wider at the top and narrower at the base. Fill each of the segments with mosaic.

SCENTED PLANTS

*Our response to smell is emotional – a scent will conjure up
the first time we smelt it and the emotions we experienced
then. Nostalgia, sadness, happiness and sensuality can all be
evoked by the scent of a flower.*

Containers are ideal for fragrant plants. In the English Country garden, pots of scented plants can be moved to positions where they will give the most pleasure – beneath the bedroom window, outside the verandah doors or next to a favourite garden seat. Many of the oldest cottage-garden plants naturally have a good perfume, although some may bear quite modest flowers. When they are combined with showier, modern hybrids there is a wealth of choice.

MIGNONETTE

Mignonette *Reseda odorata* is not much grown these days, yet it has an impressive pedigree in cottage

Dianthus barbatus 'Newport Pink'

Dianthus 'Mrs Sinkins'

and town gardens and despite its less than eye-catching looks is worth growing for its wonderful evening perfume. It first became popular in 18th-century France, where romantically minded gardeners christened it mignonette, or 'little darling', and it was soon

taken up by cottage gardeners everywhere. The sweet scent fills the garden from early summer to mid-autumn, particularly after a shower of rain, and it deserves to be more widely grown. It is an annual, easy to grow from seed each year, and needs no special

attention. It is also very attractive to bees. Because of its modest appearance the seed may not be available from your local garden centre and you may need to order it by post. Don't be put off – it really is worth the effort. When planted with showier flowers such as stocks, love-in-a-mist and nicotiana its flowers may go unnoticed, but its fragrance certainly won't.

PINKS

For perfume, look no further than the pink family, famous for their spicy, clove aroma which made them favourites for flavouring ale, wine and summer drinks. One of the oldest is *Dianthus* 'Sops-in-

Matthiola bicornis

Nicotiana 'Domino Lime'

wine', which has survived continuously since the 14th century, when it was grown in the gardens of English taverns. It has a distinctive appearance, with fringed white petals and a dark centre. For a powerful clove scent, the Victorian *D*. 'Mrs Sinkins' with its double creamy flowers is still very popular. Modern pinks (often listed as *D*. × *allwoodii*) mostly retain the perfume of their old-fashioned cousins, although traditionalists claim they can never match the older ones. The advantage of the modern forms is that they have a longer flowering period, continuing right through the summer rather than only in the early months.

To grow pinks successfully they must be in a sunny position with excellent drainage. They do well in shallow troughs, pans or sinks, grown in an alpine compost mixture made by blending two parts of loam-based compost with one part of horticultural grit. Cover the surface of the soil with gravel or stone chippings as you would for alpines. Pinks are hardy and can withstand extremes of

temperature but need protection from slugs and snails, which can cause major damage.

STOCKS

Most stocks combine pretty, long-lasting flowers with a good perfume. For evening perfume, containers should include night-scented stock (*Matthiola bicornis*), which has modest flowers but is intensely fragrant at night. Mix it with the annual Virginia stock (*Malcolmia maritima*) to combine fine flowers with fine fragrance. For daytime fragrance, cottage garden stocks (*Matthiola incana*) are popular biennials. Stocks like to be grown in full sun in a multi-

Lobularia maritima 'Orientalische Nachte'

purpose potting compost and should be watered regularly. Deadheading will extend the flowering period.

SWEET ALYSSUM

Often overlooked by container gardeners because it is traditionally used as an edging plant, the white-flowered, spreading alyssum (*Lobularia maritima*), also known as sweet Alison, has a lovely hawthorn-like scent and flowers which last virtually throughout the whole summer. It is ideal for the edge of a pot, where it will spill over the sides, attracting the bees. It is a half-hardy annual, usually bought as a bedding plant

Nicotiana 'Domino Salmon Pink'

in late spring, and is very useful for filling up spaces between more colourful plants. It likes a light, not too rich soil, ideally a gritty alpine compost, although it will survive quite well in a multi-purpose compost.

TOBACCO PLANTS

Nicotiana species and varieties are widely available as bedding plants in early summer, and can also be grown from seed. Choose the modern cultivars carefully as not all of them are scented. Note also that they are half-hardy and should not be planted out until the risk of frost is past. The species *Nicotiana* are generally too tall for containers, although they make stunning garden plants at 1–2m (4–6ft) high and if given twiggy support will look wonderful in a large tub. The Domino Series is compact at 30cm (12in) and there is a good colour range from white and lime through pinks and apricots to cerise pink. Grow in multi-purpose compost in either sun or shade and feed and deadhead regularly.

It is quite extraordinary how the most unpromising of surroundings can be quite transformed by good planting and this is particularly true of English Country style which, with its luxuriant and informal abundance, can soften hard edges and disguise unsightly features. Containers are an essential element, but the setting is also important – a featureless square patch will not become a country garden simply by positioning two or three groups of containers around it. Plant quick-growing climbers to scramble up walls and fences. Golden hop, clematis, jasmine and honeysuckle are perfect for this but never be tempted to plant the Russian vine (*Polygonum baldschuanicum*), which grows at an indecent speed and smothers all around it.

Most real English Country gardens have hedges on their boundaries rather than fences, and a hedge can be planted to disguise a boring fence, soften the appearance of the garden and provide a good backdrop for groups of containers. Hawthorn is a traditional choice. In the country it is chosen to keep out animals from neighbouring fields, but it is also a good deterrent against intruders in less rural settings as it is very thorny. It grows quickly, is easy to maintain and has wonderful flowers in late spring. If you have the space you really should plant a fruit tree – there are small varieties that do not require much

LEFT: *Here containers have been used not only to line the path but also to fill in gaps in the border for a dense cottage-garden effect.*

RIGHT: *An old kettle and a cauldron have been given a new lease of life filled with alpine dianthus and saxifrages.*

room and even some that can be grown in pots. An apple is the traditional choice, but a quince, medlar or mulberry would be a romantic and totally appropriate alternative.

A new garden shed can be improved with a tiled roof and a coat of paint or wood stain. Black stain will soon soften and give the shed the appearance of age and planting a rambling rose and a *Clematis montana* against its walls will give it added charm. Group pots of foxgloves, alchemilla and hardy geraniums either side of the door and you may be tempted to move in instead of storing your tools there!

To achieve a relaxed cottage-garden effect it is important to group a variety of containers together to create an impression of profusion, rather than dotting them randomly about the façade of the house. The planting should be soft and generous and the containers should appear to be overflowing with flowers. When grouping containers together always mix styles and sizes for a real country look. A group consisting of an old galvanized bucket, a basket, a large terracotta pot and a couple of seed pans will look much more interesting than a homogenous group of clay pots. Large containers are often the most

costly to buy, but you can achieve height in different ways: chimney-pots of different heights can be used as plinths for pots, slate or stone slabs can be raised on piles of bricks, and shelves can be fastened onto walls. This will give your garden the layered look so characteristic of English Country style.

In the true spirit of the country gardener, none of these techniques for adding height to your garden needs any real building skills – just an idea of what you want to achieve and the ability to improvise. An English Country garden is not planned and designed – it evolves as the seasons go by.

Take a relaxed approach to the containers themselves – don't worry about chips, peeling paint or broken handles as they will create just the right effect. The country gardener of earlier times would have utilized whatever containers were available – cauldrons and cooking pots no longer needed for the kitchen, cattle and horse drinking troughs, old tin buckets, baths and watering cans, wicker fruit baskets, chipped enamel bowls and jugs and wooden cider barrels. It is not necessary to be totally authentic; window boxes and hanging baskets are easier to obtain than cattle

troughs and cauldrons, and with a little imagination can be made to fit into the country look. A window box can be given a distressed paint finish or stained black and a new hanging basket will look much more informal covered with a layer of fine mesh chicken wire.

Most of us have things cluttering cupboards, attics and cellars which we just can't bring ourselves to throw out and which could become serviceable containers. An old colander lined with moss can grow alpine strawberries, a basket which has lost its handle is perfect for filling with spring bulbs and even grandad's cracked leather brogues can become quirky containers for old-fashioned pot marigolds. Old china bowls and even chamber-pots can also be used, but you should not plant directly into them because of the lack of drainage. Where a container has no drainage you should fill the base with a deep layer of gravel and stand a pot inside the container. After exceptionally heavy rain it may be necessary to empty out excess water.

If your attic is bare and your cupboards are clutter-free you will need to raid your local junk shops and garage and car boot sales for suitable containers. You are unlikely to find real garden antiques as these days they fetch high prices, but old galvanized baths and buckets, chipped enamelware, tatty baskets and wooden crates can still be picked up for next to nothing. These days you will be lucky to buy a stone sink cheaply, but a

glazed china sink can look pretty when planted. Go with an open mind – the most unlikely objects can become charming when overflowing with plants and it doesn't really matter if their life is limited when you have spent very little obtaining them. Some of the prettiest objects are decrepit to the point of disintegration and you wouldn't dream of taking them into your home, but they look wonderful in the garden even if for just one season.

Reclamation yards and scrapyards can also be fruitful sources of large containers. An old galvanized water tank can make a surprisingly successful planter, although it will need to have holes drilled in the base for drainage. A container such as this is ideal for tumbling and climbing plants, especially when it is positioned against a wall. Combine a repeat-flowering climbing rose such as 'New Dawn' or 'Climbing Iceberg' with a ground cover rose such as 'Nozomi', *Lavandula angustifolia* 'Hidcote' and *Rosemarinus officinalis* 'Miss Jessop's Upright' and the water tank will soon be overflowing with abundant flowers and foliage. Look out as well for industrial scrap such as old crucibles and cast-iron pipes and hoppers, which can have a new lease of life in the garden.

LEFT: *An enamel chamber-pot can enjoy a happy retirement as a container for grape hyacinths (*Muscari*).*

RIGHT: *Set prettily among plants in the border, a mosaic pot is filled with white petunias.*

Although exchanging plants with friends and neighbours is one of the nicest and most inexpensive ways of obtaining plants, you may not have obliging neighbours or garden enthusiast friends, in which case you will need to look elsewhere. Cottage-garden plants are enduringly popular, so you will probably be able to buy a reasonable selection at your local garden centre, but it is much more fun, and in the spirit of this style of gardening, to search out specialist nurseries and patronize local flower shows and plant sales.

There are many lovely perennials which are worth looking out for, all of which will contribute to English Country containers. *Alchemilla mollis* is a classic cottage-garden plant, with its inverted umbrella-shaped leaves which hold droplets of moisture like beads of mercury on their surface and its fine sprays of tiny lime green flowers. It is a wonderfully easy plant to grow and is perfectly happy in a container. Once it is established in your garden you will never be without it and neither need your friends be, because it will seed freely and you will have lots of plants to give away. Leave some seedlings to establish themselves in paths, wall

LEFT: *Pinks and pelargoniums are traditional cottage-garden favourites which can be grown easily from cuttings.*

RIGHT: *Old-fashioned plants like the sweet william (*Dianthus barbatus*) are an essential component of the English country garden.*

crevices and around the base of containers. Another wonderfully easy plant is the columbine, or aquilegia. *Aquilegia vulgaris* is the common form, sometimes known as 'Granny's Bonnet', which self-seeds everywhere with a range of flower colours from white through pink to deep blue.

The perennial cornflower (*Centaurea cyanus*) will grow happily in a large tub, but it does need to be cut back to new growth after flowering or it can look very tatty. It is best grown in among other plants such as red valerian (*Centranthus ruber*), another strong-growing perennial which is suitable for large pots or tubs. Cornflower will grow happily in the poorest of soils, needing little attention to flower all summer long, as will valerian (*Valeriana*), yellow loosestrife (*Lysimachia punctata*) and purple loosestrife (*Lythrum salicaria*).

The yellow fumitory (*Corydalis lutea*) is so easy to grow that it is sometimes thought of as a weed, but this is not fair as it is a lovely, delicate plant which will gratefully grow in any shady corner you choose to place it in and will soon colonize surrounding cracks and crevices.

No cottage garden is complete without catmint (*Nepeta*), its soft silvery-grey foliage and mauvey-blue flowers creating a haze of gentle colour. As its name suggests, it is beloved by cats, who will destroy it in their passion to rub against the foliage. Stand your pot of catmint on top of a chimney-pot

where its flowers can be seen to best advantage and it is protected from marauding felines.

Lamb's ears (*Stachys byzantina*) is one of the most tactile of plants, with its velvety leaves covered in a deep pile of silvery hairs. In summer the mat of leaves is topped by spikes of pinky-mauve flowers. Grow it on its own in a wide, shallow container and cut it back quite hard in the autumn to keep it under control.

When one thinks of English Country-style containers it is inevitable that one pictures them in high summer, but the other seasons should not be neglected. With a little planning it is possible to have something interesting growing all the year round, and by planting some of the containers with evergreens you will create a setting for flowering plants whatever the season. Rosemary is a fine traditional choice and its beautiful blue flowers appear from mid-winter onwards. The cotton lavender (*Santolina chamaecyparissus*) retains its silvery foliage in a moderate climate and can be clipped into a smooth ball-shape as can the ever-reliable box plant (*Buxus*). Ivies will grow prolifically in containers and a pot of variegated ivy will lighten a gloomy corner at any time of year.

In the depths of winter, winter pansies can be relied on for colour, and even though they may appear to be laid low by heavy frost or snow they will cheerfully carry on blooming as soon as better weather returns. At the start of the year, place pots of snowdrops and aconites on a windowsill or on a ledge near the door where they can be admired as you pass by. Plant one or two larger pots with hellebores (*Helleborus orientalis*) to flower from midwinter. Place them on top of a wall or on a ledge where you can see the beautiful flowers without having to stoop. Spring bulbs are an obvious choice, especially the smaller varieties,

which can be arranged in a tabletop display. Bulbs should ideally be planted in the autumn but young plants can also be bought in the spring, although they will be more expensive. Wallflowers should also be planted in autumn – it may seem a thankless task when you are filling a tub with them on a bleak day, but the colour and scent in the spring makes it well worth the effort.

There is a long tradition of growing auriculas in English country gardens and they look their best planted individually in old terracotta pots. Grouped together on a tabletop or windowledge in partial shade they will enchant all who see them. After they have flowered they should be stood in a cool corner of the garden for the summer. Divide them in early summer – each plant will separate into a number of plantlets to pot up individually. Keep well fed and watered during the growing season and protect from slugs and snails.

The period from late spring to midsummer is a time of profusion in the English country garden, but plants can start to look rather tired and straggly in late summer. Regular feeding, trimming and deadheading will help prevent this and you can lengthen the flowering season of many container plants by cutting back half of the growth after the first flush of flowers. This will give the plants a rest and encourage new shoots to grow from the base of the stems.

Many summer plants will continue flowering right up until the first frosts

LEFT: *In 18th-century England the growing of auriculas (*Primula auricula*) was a serious pastime, with prize-winning specimens changing hands for large sums of money.*

BELOW: *Auriculas look best grown in individual terracotta pots.*

and this is especially true of the flowers which really don't get going until midsummer, such as dahlias, zinnias, the half-hardy salvias and sedums. All will do well grown in containers in full sun. As autumn frosts approach put half-hardy plants you wish to save for next year somewhere frost-free and replace them with pots of hardy cyclamen, heathers and ericas which, along with your evergreen plants, will keep your containers colourful right through to the end of the year.

The old horse or cattle trough was probably one of the first containers that country people used for their plants. Wooden and stone troughs and butler's sinks have become a feature of cottage gardens over the centuries as a way of re-creating the garden in miniature with small forms of cottage-garden favourites such as aquilegias, campanulas, pinks and phlox. Troughs also make good deep containers for climbing roses, honeysuckle and jasmine or for scented geraniums, herbs and butterfly plants like sedum and buddleia. Just because they have become known as alpine troughs does not mean that alpine plants are the only ones that will look the part.

Stone troughs are expensive and increasingly rare, but reconstituted stone versions are cheaper and weather well in a season or two. New timber troughs made in the old manger or cradle style are also well suited to cottage-garden plants. Old glazed china sinks don't need to be disguised or given a stone cladding, as they often are in suburban gardens. With judicious planting the foliage and flowers will soon spill over the sides and soften the whiteness.

Decide on a permanent site for your trough before it is planted – an empty trough can be heavy and difficult to move, but filled with soil and plants it becomes well-nigh impossible. Position it where it will get a reasonable amount of sunlight – at least half the day. Most plants suited to growing in troughs prefer an open, sunny position so you should also make sure there are no overhanging trees or shrubs that will cast too much shade. Raise the trough off the ground with bricks, stone blocks or even an old sewing-machine stand. Ideally choose a site against a wall, under a window or freestanding in a courtyard or on a patio. If the trough is against the wall of a house, make sure water will not run off the eaves or a windowsill into the trough as this could wash away the compost and damage flowers and foliage.

The traditional trough is usually planted with perennials rather than a new display each year and for this purpose you should fill your container with a compost which is a mix of 2 parts loam-based compost such as John Innes No. 2, 2 parts standard potting compost and 1 part coarse grit. This mix has good moisture retention in dry weather but is also free-draining so it does not become waterlogged in wet conditions. When planting the trough, scatter slow-release plant-food granules on the surface and topdress with these each spring. Before filling the trough with compost, cover the plug hole with a crumpled piece of wire mesh and spread broken crocks across the base. Once you have planted the trough, cover the soil with a generous layer of gravel or limestone chippings.

RIGHT: *Including rocks among the plants in your stone trough will give it the appearance of a miniature landscape.*

Annual flowers have traditionally taken a central role in the English Country garden. Thrifty cottage gardeners collect seed from their own plants each year and exchange surpluses with friends and neighbours. It is easy to save your own seed and the pleasure of filling your garden with free colour is one to be savoured. To collect seed you will need to be less scrupulous about deadheading and leave the sometimes unsightly seedheads to ripen fully on the plant before they are harvested. Choose a dry day and as soon as you pick each stem of seedheads place it head downwards into a paper bag on which you have written the plant name. Tie the neck of the bag tightly with string and leave it somewhere warm but well ventilated to allow the seeds to finish ripening. Shake the bag occasionally and when you can hear the seeds rattling free of the seedheads they can be removed and packed into labelled self-seal plastic bags. Start with really easy seeds like marigolds (*Calendula*), foxgloves, sweet peas and love-in-a-mist.

Sowing and growing annual seeds is very easy in most cases and as a general rule the larger the seed is the easier it is to grow; as with all rules there are exceptions, but marigolds, sunflowers, sweet peas and nasturtiums are good choices for the beginner to start with. Try to be restrained with the number of seeds you sow, as when you are growing plants for containers the number you require will be limited. Use 10cm (4in) or 15cm (6in) pots rather than seed trays. With large seeds sow just six per pot, and with fine seed mix the seed with silver sand to help you sow thinly. This isn't just a matter of economy – you will get better germination and healthier plants if they aren't too crowded. A mixture of 50/50 potting compost and vermiculite, available at garden centres, is a very good growing medium. Large seeds can be pushed into the compost, but fine seeds should be sprinkled on the surface and covered only with a single layer of vermiculite granules. Water well and stand in a warm, dark place until germination has taken place, when they can be moved to a light position.

Seedlings should be pricked out into larger pots as soon as their first pair of proper leaves has developed. Feed them regularly until they are ready to be planted out – proprietary composts have only six weeks of food in them, after which your plants will starve without additional feeding.

Some annuals do best if they are not moved after sowing, so check the seed packet for instructions. Among others, love-in-a-mist, night-scented stocks, Californian poppies and the poached-egg plant fall into this category. However, it isn't always practicable to sow them directly into the containers as these will usually still be filled with spring flowers at this stage. Instead, sow the seeds into peat pots. After

ABOVE: *A basket planted with asters and trailing antirrhinums will flower profusely from midsummer onwards.*

LEFT: *A mixed border of annuals and perennials supplemented by container planting creates a tapestry of colour.*

germination thin the seedlings, leaving the three strongest. They can then be planted out, still in the peat pots, when your containers become free for summer planting. Young plants should always be transplanted in their final position well before they come into flower or they will tend to be thin and straggly.

Woodland

A shady corner of the garden is often considered to be a difficult area, but when it is filled with a selection of containers planted with shade-loving plants it can become an asset instead of a liability, a cool haven on hot summer days.

WOODLAND STYLE takes its inspiration from two sources: the forests of the northern hemisphere, where close-ranked pine trees filter the light and litter the ground with their needles and cones, and log cabins nestle in clearings at the end of forest rides; and from deciduous lowland woods and copses where oak, beech, silver birch, ash, sycamore and maple grow alongside one another, their green canopy sheltering woodland plants from the strong light of summer but allowing light through from autumn leaf fall to spring when the green haze of new growth unfurls into leaves.

It is possible to re-create the tranquillity of a woodland setting wherever you live, and it is particularly suitable for shady corners of the garden where the choice of plants is more challenging than usual. Containers can be constructed from typical forest byproducts such as unsawn timber and hollowed-out logs, decorated with twigs, bark, moss and cones. Plants are chosen which reflect this cool woodland atmosphere: ferns, foxgloves, bluebells, primroses and violets all thrive in the low light levels.

Woodland style is very informal; plants should be allowed to climb and tumble with only the barest interference when they threaten to get out of hand. Seedheads should be left on the plants to encourage self-seeding and allow nature to have an increasing influence on the design. Young seedlings will appear in neighbouring pots and also in any crevices on paths and at the base of walls. Mosses are to be encouraged; in damp corners with low light they will colonize brick paths, flagstones, the surfaces of containers and any spot left undisturbed. Birds, insects and butterflies will appreciate this style of gardening, which provides them with both food and shelter. Like the forests and woods on which it is based, a woodland garden is at its best in spring and autumn. In the height of summer it can look rather monochromatic, although a planting of ferns will provide interest from early spring right through to late autumn.

LEFT: *Bluebells (*Hyacinthoides non-scripta*) and alpine strawberries (*Fragaria vesca*) thrive in woodland shade.*

RIGHT: *Planters made from stacked rustic logs soon blend into the wild garden when filled with woodland flowers.*

Craft Project 6

MOSS AND TWIG POT COVERS

YOU WILL NEED

• A 3.5 litre (7in) plastic pot
• Green plastic-coated garden wire
• Secateurs or wire-cutters
• A small saw
• A hand or electric drill

As MUCH AS we would all love to fill our gardens with old, weathered terracotta pots, sometimes we have to make do with plastic. This twig and moss cover will disguise the plainest of plastic pots.

Construction

1. Use the saw to cut the twigs, varying the lengths and the angle of cutting – the cover will not have as much charm if the twigs are too regular.
2. Lay the twigs next to one another and drill a hole in each 30mm (1¼in) from the base and another hole 125mm (5in) from the first.
3. Thread the wire through the holes and cut, leaving a generous length at each end.
4. Pack the spaces between the twigs with sphagnum moss, keeping the wires fairly taut to hold the moss in place. Don't worry if some moss won't stay in place – it can be pushed back once the cover is in position around the pot.
5. Lay the pot centrally on the moss and twigs and pull the cover around the pot. At this stage you may need to add or remove a twig or two for a snug fit.
6. Once the cover is the correct size, join the wires together by twisting them tightly around one another, trim the ends to 50mm (2in) and tuck them behind the moss.

TO DECORATE

• 20 twigs of approximately 25mm (1in) diameter and 200–250mm (8–10in) length
• Sphagnum moss

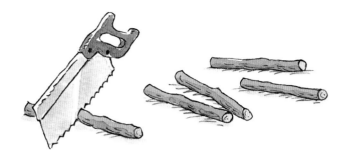

1. Use the saw to cut 20 twigs of approximately the same length.

2. Drill holes in each twig 30mm (1¼in) from the base and 125mm (5in) from the first hole.

3. Thread wire through the holes. To prevent the twigs from sliding along the wire, wrap the top wire round one side of each twig and pass it through the hole again.

4. Pack the spaces between the twigs with moss.

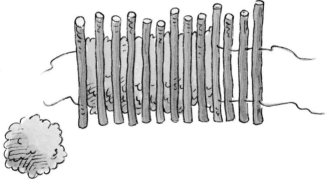

5. Lay the pot on the twigs, with the half turns of the top wire against the pot, and pull the cover around the pot before fastening the wires to hold it in place.

Gathering Moss

If you have a very mossy garden you can collect your own, and if your lawn is more moss than grass it will benefit from its removal. However, you should never gather moss from forests or woods, where it is an important food and habitat for wild life. Bags of sphagnum moss are available from garden centres and florists.

Looking After Your Pot Cover

A pot cover made from these materials has a limited life, but it will certainly last the season and possibly longer if it is dried off and kept in a dark, well-ventilated place over winter.

Plant Profile

FERNS

Ferns are the perfect choice for a shady garden with a woodland feel to it. They are very easy to grow, particularly in containers, where they can be given a cool, moist environment which might not be possible in an open border.

Many people have the impression that ferns are specialist plants, not for the average gardener. In fact, the only difference between ferns and other plants is in the way they reproduce – by spores held on the underside of leaves, rather than by seed – but this is only relevant if you want to propagate them. Otherwise they behave pretty much like other foliage plants, although the foliage is referred to as fronds rather than leaves. They can be kept in pots for years and years, providing some permanent greenery in those corners of the garden where many flowering plants would not survive. Some ferns are evergreen and keep their leaves all year, others are deciduous and die back in winter. All the species and cultivars mentioned here are hardy in temperate climates and unless stated otherwise can stay outdoors all the year round. Ferns are relatively slow-growing plants, so they are ideal for permanent plantings which will need little attention for many years.

As a general rule, ferns look better planted individually, one to a

Polystichum aculeatum

pot. Alternatively, three or more plants can be grouped together in a long trough or, in large barrels, they can be combined with foxgloves or bluebells. The two most popular ferns sold in garden centres are the male fern *Dryopteris filix-mas* and the female fern *Athyrium filix-femina*. To grow either of these you will need a large wooden barrel as they can easily reach 1m (3¼ft) across. Both have the classic arching fronds and feathery foliage, although the female fern is paler in colour and has a slightly less robust appearance. In winter the female fern will disappear altogether, leaving just a central crown, while the fronds of the male fern will turn colour but may well stay on the plant until new fronds unfurl in the spring. The male fern has a close relative, *Dryopteris erythrosa*, which is known as the copper shield fern because of its colourful fronds. The young fronds start a pinkish-red, turn to burnished copper and eventually mature to a deep green. It is more compact than the male fern, reaching about 45cm (18in) high and wide, and looks wonderful grown individually in terracotta pots.

The maidenhair fern (*Adiantum pedatum*) is probably better known as a houseplant, but it is fairly hardy outdoors and grows well in a small container. It has black stems and lime-green fronds which will eventually grow to a height

Polystichum setiferum

Adiantum pedatum 'Imbricatum'

Success with Ferns

Most ferns like moist conditions and hate it if their roots dry out. Add water-retaining gel to the compost when planting and stand the pots on gravel-filled saucers from spring until late autumn. Mulch the top of the pots, troughs or barrels with a layer of composted leafmould or bark chippings. This will help keep the roots cool and retain moisture.

Ferns have a very fine, shallow root system and dislike being disturbed. Only repot in spring and summer when they are actively growing and can adapt most easily to the change.

Ferns do not need much feeding, and an annual topdressing with slow-release plant food granules will be sufficient.

Leave old fronds in place overwinter to protect the crown. Snip off in spring when new growth begins.

and spread of about 40cm (16 in). The maidenhair fern dies back in winter and if possible should be put into an outhouse or porch to protect it against the frost.

Probably the largest group of garden ferns are the aspleniums, which include the well-known harts-tongue fern (*Asplenium scolopendrium*) and the spleenworts, all of which are evergreen. The harts-tongue is one of the bigger ferns and will need a fairly substantial pot. The fronds are not dissected like other ferns, but are simple straps of green (rather like a tongue), eventually

reaching 60cm (2ft) in length. The harts-tongue is one of the few ferns that can stand some drying out as its natural habitat is rock crevices where the water supply can be erratic. The spleenworts are among the smaller members of the asplenium group and are ideal for small pots and window boxes.

The black spleenwort (*Asplenium adiantum-nigrum*) and the common spleenwort (*Asplenium trichomanes*) reach a height and spread of around 30cm (12in) and are very adaptable to sun, shade, damp or dry conditions – ideal for those who tend to forget their plants. All the asplenium group are happiest

in a lime-rich soil, but they will adapt to an ordinary loam-based compost.

Two more evergreen ferns well worth growing in pots are the polystichums, or shield ferns. The soft-shield fern (*Polystichum setiferum*) grows to a substantial 1m (3^1/$_4$ft) and has the classic highly dissected fern foliage which lasts all year round. There are several smaller forms such as the dwarf Congestum group. The hard-shield fern (*P. aculeatum*) is a mid-sized plant, about 45cm (18in) high and wide, with glossy dark green fronds.

Athyrium filix-femina

Asplenium scolopendrium

Dryopteris erythrosora

Dryopteris filix-mas 'Fred Jackson'

Given the choice, most of us would probably opt for a sunny, south-facing garden. In reality, few of us have that and yet we persist with trying to grow plants which need these conditions. This tends to be unsatisfactory for both garden and gardener alike; it is far better to grow plants which will thrive in their setting. 'Woodland' is a romantic way of describing any dark, damp, shady and difficult area which has the potential to be transformed by containers filled with plants which enjoy cool, moist shade. It may be a corner of the garden shaded by trees, the foot of a north-facing wall, a narrow alleyway where the sun never penetrates or a neglected basement area. Woodland style can be applied to all these situations by using barrels, troughs and pots planted with shade-loving plants, many of which will need little attention once they are established.

Of all garden conditions, perhaps the trickiest is the dry shade which often exists under mature trees. Only the heaviest rain penetrates the leaf canopy and the soil is impoverished because the tree takes up all the available nutrients. In a small town garden, the entire garden can be affected in this way by a tree which isn't even within the boundaries. Woodland-style containers are a solution in these conditions, with shade-loving plants planted into a moisture-retentive compost. Grouped together, a number of containers will create a lush effect and be less prone to drying out. Anyone who chooses to garden with containers is aware that regular watering is essential and this is certainly true of containers stood in dry shade, but with regular watering and occasional feeding there is no reason why these plants should not thrive.

The setting for woodland containers should ideally be suitably rustic. If the budget allows, lay paths or a patio with

old bricks and replace ordinary fencing with woven willow or hazel panels. A cheaper alternative to brick paving is to line the path or patio along its edges with logs and fill the centre with a thick layer of chipped bark, although this would not be practical close to the house where chippings may be trailed indoors. Cut lengths of railway sleepers make very good steps, but each one should be covered with fine-mesh chicken wire to prevent them from becoming slippery. The wire mesh will quickly weather down and become nearly invisible.

In the absence of a log cabin, paint the garden shed a soft grey-green colour which will age beautifully. Decorate the external walls of the shed with broken garden tools and other interesting pieces of junk and stand large logs on end near the door and along the side walls as plinths for planted pots. Piles of cut logs neatly stacked against the walls will emphasize the theme, provide shelter for all sorts of beneficial garden insects and maybe even tempt a hedgehog to take up residence. Fix nesting boxes well out of reach of the neighbourhood cats and suspend bird feeders from overhead branches or wall brackets – a woodland garden is all the more charming when it has its resident birds.

LEFT: *A dark corner of the garden can be brought to life by the inclusion of a basket planted with woodland flowers.*

RIGHT: *Stately cream foxgloves (Digitalis) bring a splash of light to shady woodland.*

I f you go down to the woods today you will find heaps of inspiration to take home with you, but you should not strip the woodland of its bounty in the process. Nowadays many woodlands and forests are protected and it is illegal to take anything at all away with you, but even in unregulated areas you should act with restraint. You can check on the status of your local woodlands and forests by enquiring at your library.

We may view pine cones as pretty decorative objects, but to many woodland creatures they are an important source of food, both the pine nuts and the cones themselves, so take a few and leave plenty behind. Loose bark on fallen trees can have beautiful markings, ideal for embellishing a wooden trough or planter, but in the natural world it provides home and shelter for many insects, so don't strip it off indiscriminately. As tempting as they

are, mosses should never be gathered from the wild: they provide food for many creatures and help prevent erosion of the woodland floor. Woodland plants and flowers may not be dug from the wild, and in some instances it is also illegal to collect seed, but garden centres and specialist nurseries stock wildflower plants and seeds which come from authorized sources.

But don't regard a walk in the woods as a frustrating temptation; look around you instead and notice the miniature still lives which reveal themselves at every step – here a tussock of moss cushioning the fallen flowers from a foxglove, there a clump of violets nestled up against a decaying log – as the way plants grow in their natural surroundings can provide a rich source of inspiration for your woodland containers. By adding this sort of detail to your containers you will achieve a much more naturalistic look.

Even the smallest garden has a corner where you can stack decorative bits and pieces that will add character and authenticity to your woodland containers. A few logs and terracotta pots tucked in a damp spot between the shed and the fence or left overwinter underneath a shrub will be colonized by algae and mosses. Christmas bulbs such as hyacinths and narcissus often come with bun moss or carpet moss tucked around the bulbs. Don't leave it to dry out when the bulbs have finished flowering – spread the moss on a layer of damp peat in a seed tray and stand it in a shady corner of the garden until you are ready to use it for your woodland pots.

When you are pruning the shrubs in your garden keep the twiggy branches.

LEFT: *A seed pan planted with snowdrops* (Galanthus) *and cyclamen uses moss as a decoration and to prevent soil splashing on foliage and flowers.*

RIGHT: Cymbalaria muralis *and* Viola labradorica *tumble in profusion from a pot tucked in a cool, shady corner.*

Bundle them together and hang them up ready to use as supports for tall-growing plants like foxgloves, Solomon's seal and martagon lilies; twigs look so much more natural than canes and string, and hung in bundles from the eaves of the shed they add decoration while they wait to be used. If your garden doesn't have the right sort of twiggy branches ask neighbours to save you some when they do their pruning, or approach the gardener at your local park – other gardeners are nearly always happy to help.

Containers for the woodland-style garden can be as simple as a collection of weathered terracotta pots, or log-cabin-style rustic troughs and planters made from rough timber offcuts and split logs. Really old terracotta is becoming increasingly scarce and expensive, especially the larger pots, but you can still find the occasional bargain, usually where a pot or two is mixed in with a box of assorted junk. Buying pieces one at a time like this from junk shops, rather than antique shops, is a good way of building a collection. Pots don't need to be antique to develop a weathered look – you can plant up new pots and leave them in a damp, shady spot, where they will develop mosses and algae fairly quickly. You can speed up the process by painting them with seaweed plant food diluted 50/50 with water, or a similar dilution of fresh cow manure should you have access to it and the inclination to handle it.

Logs and timber offcuts can be used to make large inexpensive planters which will fit well into a woodland landscape. At their most basic they can consist of two parallel logs laid on the ground to define the front and back of the planter, on to which are stacked two more logs at right angles to define the sides. The logs are nailed together where they intersect. This process is repeated until the desired height is achieved. The gaps between the logs are filled with smaller logs and mosses.

Planted with foxgloves (*Digitalis*), bluebells (*Hyacinthoides non-scripta*), periwinkles (*Vinca major*) and other woodland plants, they will quickly mellow and become part of the landscape. This type of container cannot be moved, but it should last about five years before you need to renew it.

Wooden crates and boxes can be embellished with rustic timber to make woodland planters. Timber mills and wood yards often have bins of timber offcuts which can be bought very cheaply, including pieces of wood with the bark still attached. Cut down and nailed into position they will give the box a very rustic appearance. A more sophisticated version of this style of decoration takes its inspiration from the

Tyrol, where log cabins were decorated inside and out with mosaic-type patterns of twigs, pine cones and nuts. For this style of decoration, outline each side of the box with rustic twigs and fill the central area with patterns of cones, nuts and more twigs. The larger pieces can be tacked into position and the smaller ones glued in place.

Any wooden planter, trough or window box will have the right look if it is made from rough or weathered timber. When visiting your local wood yard ignore the stacks of newly cut symmetrical timber and look around for irregular pieces, especially rustic poles with or without their bark. With basic carpentry skills these can be turned into simple planters. If even basic carpentry is beyond you, you may find that you can buy this sort of wooden box from country garden centres, farm shops and timber mills. They are often painted with wood preservative in a rather unpleasant orange-brown colour, but a coat of dark brown wood stain will improve their appearance enormously.

Rustic baskets woven from vines are attractive, if relatively short-lived, containers for the woodland garden, but as they are inexpensive to buy they can be replaced when they reach the point of disintegration.

ABOVE: *A tiny basket holds a shade-loving busy lizzie (*Impatiens*).*

RIGHT: *Many woodland plants grow well in containers provided they are in shade for part of the day.*

The successful woodland-style garden looks as if all the plants have colonized the area of their own accord, even in the containers. It is gardening at its most natural-looking, but we all know that left to its own devices the garden would probably grow little more than nettles, chickweed and docks. The trick is to introduce plants, but grow them in conditions as close to their natural habitat as possible. Use shallow pans and half pots for small woodland plants like primroses and violets, as they look far better in these than in taller pots. Group smaller containers around the larger ones so that the impression given is of layers of plants rather than neat rows, and cover the soil around the plants with small pine cones, bun moss and lichen-encrusted twigs.

By planting a selection of bulbs and plants in containers of various sizes you can create your own woodland glade to delight you all year round. At the very beginning of the year when little else is growing, the first snowdrops (*Galanthus nivalis*) and winter aconites (*Eranthis hyemalis*) will appear in the gloom, soon to be followed by the beautiful hellebore *Helleborus orientalis*. In early spring, the woodland garden is at its

ABOVE: *Most woodland plants look their best in spring and early summer, but regular deadheading will encourage plants like hardy geraniums and tolmiea to keep on flowering.*

LEFT: *A basket of ferns and ivy hung from a branch of a tree will look good all year.*

best and there is colour everywhere. Plant the white wood anemone *Anemone nemerosa* and one of its blue cultivars. Primroses (*Primula vulgaris*), violets (*Viola odorata*) and miniature daffodils such as *Narcissus* 'Hawera' or *N*. 'February Gold' will look delightful in a large, shallow container with the purple-leaved *Viola labradorica*. A window box for a shady sill can be filled with lilies-of-the-valley (*Convallaria majalis*), which are deliciously scented.

No woodland garden is complete without bluebells (*Hyacinthoides non-scripta*). It is now illegal to dig them from the wild, but ask among your friends – anyone who has them established in the garden will be only too happy to let you have some bulbs, as they tend to be prolific to the point of pestilential in the herbaceous border! Otherwise they can be bought from

nurseries – never be tempted to buy them from market stalls or car boot sales as they will almost certainly have been dug from the wild and this trade should be discouraged.

The stately foxglove *Digitalis purpurea* is among the most beautiful of woodland plants, and in a good year it will carpet the woodland floor with colourful spires. Foxgloves adapt well to containers and will seed themselves everywhere provided you leave the stems in place until the seed is dry. Once you can hear the seeds rattling, shake them wherever you want them to grow and by the autumn you should have seedlings everywhere.

By midsummer most woodland plants will have finished flowering, but your containers can still look good if you introduce other shade-loving plants such as variegated hostas, *Dicentra eximia* with its delicate pink heart-shaped flowers, the dead-nettles *Lamium galeobdolon* and *L. maculatum* 'Beacon Silver' and the colourful, tender *Coleus blumei*. The autumn-flowering cyclamens such as *Cyclamen hederifolium* or *C. cyprium* will push their bright pink flowers through a carpet of autumn leaves and bring a splash of late colour to your woodland containers.

Most woodland plants prefer to grow in an acid compost, although they will tolerate standard commercial composts which have a small amount of lime. They will benefit from a mulch of leafmould or shredded bark.

Anyone who has a cool, shady garden will know that while the conditions may encourage lush green growth, they also encourage inordinate numbers of voracious slugs and snails who will munch through the greenery at an alarming rate. It is very disheartening to have the beautiful leaves of your favourite hosta reduced

FAR LEFT: *Erythroniums are elegant woodland flowers which grow well in containers.*

MAIN PICTURE, LEFT: *A collection of ferns at the foot of a tree creates a woodland feel in the centre of a lawn.*

to filigree work overnight, or worse still to find that a clump of delicate erythroniums on the brink of flowering have disappeared entirely.

Pest control is an important aspect of the woodland-style garden, and how you go about it depends really on how squeamish you are. The ruthless (author included) find that regular patrols wearing heavy boots are very effective. Slug pellets undoubtedly work, but although they contain an additive to repel pets, there is the danger that songbirds such as blackbirds or thrushes may eat poisoned snails. Saucers of beer certainly attract slugs and snails who presumably die happy, but you are left with a disgusting brew and the dilemma of where to dispose of it. The sentimental gardener can collect the slugs and snails and release them in the wild, but should note that 'the wild' does not mean next door's garden or the local park. Physical barriers can also be effective in some circumstances – a 2.5cm (1in) band of petroleum jelly smeared just below the rim of a pot is said to deter slugs and snails and similarly a copper wire wrapped around the pot is reported to deliver a shock which stops them in their tracks. With either of these methods it is essential that the foliage of the plant does not

touch the sides of the pot below the barrier and also that it does not touch foliage in adjoining pots or the slugs and snails will simply take a detour around the barrier.

One of the best and most positive ways to control pests in your garden is to encourage beneficial wildlife. A resident hedgehog will snuffle out slugs and snails, but it will need an undisturbed corner of the garden to live in – a pile of logs is a favourite home, or you could try a purpose-built hedgehog house as these are now being offered at some garden centres and in mail-order catalogues. Frogs and toads will also do their bit; you don't have to have a pond in your garden for them to live in it, but it does help. Songbirds like trees, hedges and thickets, and if your garden has any of these they will happily scratch about among your plants rooting out the slugs and snails.

An alternative approach to the pest problem is to grow plants which slugs and snails don't eat. They appear to have no interest in ferns, the only damage they cause being the trail they leave behind them as they traverse the fronds in search of something more palatable. Ivies remain untouched, as do day-lilies (*Hemerocallis*) and hellebores. Filling all your containers with plants that slugs and snails don't like would make for a rather dull display, but a good proportion of resistant plants will ensure that you can better look after the more vulnerable specimens.

Faded Splendour

Faded Splendour finds its inspiration

in an earlier age when gardening was

on a grand scale. Containers

which were objects of beauty in their own

right overflowed with lush plantings

to magnificent effect and

conservatories were filled with exotic

and fragrant flowers.

THERE IS A romance to the neglected, overgrown garden which appeals to all of us. Maybe it is the images we have carried in our heads since childhood when we first heard the story of Sleeping Beauty which makes us imagine that behind every tangled climbing rose and overgrown shrub lies something magical. The wonderful reality is that in some cases it is true – the gardens of Heligan in Cornwall were forgotten and neglected for most of the 20th century but are now delighting admiring visitors as more and more of their mysteries are revealed and they are replanted in the grand style of their earlier glory. Of course few of us have gardens on this scale and the best most of us can manage is a neglected corner near the garden shed filled with nothing more romantic than broken pots and empty compost sacks, but the same principles apply – you can make something beautiful from something neglected.

Faded Splendour is for the romantic gardener who prefers old-fashioned varieties of plants, collects old garden tools as objects of beauty and loves the appearance of weathered wood and faded paintwork. Not for this

gardener the bowling-green lawn with immaculate edges and serried ranks of brightly coloured annuals. Although it will be more of a challenge, even a new garden can take some of the elements of Faded Splendour and use them to give the space character, but be careful not to overdo it or it may end up looking like a Disney 'theme' garden instead of a romantic re-creation of an earlier style of gardening.

The number of antique pots and statues (or good replicas) which find their way into more modest gardens shows how much in vogue this look is. Lead troughs which have seen better days, stone urns ravaged by time, filigree metalwork arches and bowers and huge earthenware pots chipped and cracked by years of use all have an inherent beauty. To complement these timeless pieces, make the planting big and bold. This approach will be perfect if you have a larger garden or simply want to make a definite statement with a few well-chosen containers.

LEFT: *A magnificent antique urn needs little embellishment to draw the eye.*

RIGHT: *A Victorian log store becomes a mysterious grotto with the help of a hanging basket and pots of ferns and lilies.*

Craft Project 7

VERDIGRIS POTS

YOU WILL NEED

• A terracotta pot, preferably
with a rough surface
• A paintbrush
• Medium-grade sandpaper
• Sheets of newspaper

IDEALLY, FOR a garden with faded splendour your containers should have the patina of age. In the absence of a decade or two to spare, or the funds to buy antique pieces, it is sometimes necessary to employ a bit of deception. Paint finishes which are hugely popular indoors can also be used outdoors to give your containers the illusion of age, as has been done with these verdigris pots.

Construction

1. Before decorating the pot ensure that it is clean and dry. Brush on a coat of the blue-green paint and leave to dry fully.

2. Now paint a coat of the off-white emulsion over the blue-green. Use the brush nearly dry to achieve a very light covering. (Remove the excess paint by brushing it onto a sheet of newspaper until only a little paint remains on the brush.) Allow to dry.

3. Use your finger to apply thin patches of gilt wax randomly. You can do this wearing rubber gloves if you don't like getting your hands dirty.

4. Finally, rub the pot back with sandpaper to encourage the different colours of paint and the gilt wax to blend and soften. In places rub right back to the terracotta as this will enhance the aged look.

TO DECORATE

• Blue-green emulsion paint
• Off-white emulsion paint
• A pot or tube of gilt wax
(available from art shops)

1. Brush on a coat of blue-green paint and leave to dry.

2. Apply a light coat of off-white paint by using a nearly dry brush. Remove excess paint by brushing onto newspaper.

3. Use your finger to apply patches of gilt wax randomly.

4. Gently rub back the pot with sandpaper to blend and soften the paint colours and wax.

True Verdigris

Real verdigris is actually a green rust which forms on copper and bronze, eventually turning the entire surface a beautiful pale blue-green. To encourage it on statuary and containers in the garden, spray them with vinegar or include them when you are spraying liquid feed on to your plants as something in the feed helps the verdigris to form.

Ageing New Terracotta

To tone down the bright red colour of new terracotta, paint the surface with a coat of liquid seaweed plant food diluted 50/50 with water. Not only will this soften the colour, it will also promote the growth of algae.

LILIES

No other flower lends an air of faded splendour more evocatively than the lily, with the apparently conflicting combination of exoticism and purity that their blooms convey. However, most varieties are surprisingly easy to grow.

Lilies are among the most beautiful of plants. They bring dignity to the garden and lend even the newest of gardens an air of grandeur. Perhaps this derives from the fact that lilies are among the oldest plants in cultivation. Madonna lilies (*Lilium candidum*) are depicted on Cretan vases from the Minoan period (1700BC), were known to the Phoenicians and the Romans and were later adopted as a symbol of Christian purity. Despite all this history, the real romance of the lily lies in its incomparable scent. Fortunately this scent is not confined to the Madonna lily, which is undoubtedly classically beautiful in looks and perfume, but can be difficult to grow. Unlike most other lilies it should be planted with its bulbs only just below the surface and it make take two or three years to establish.

There are hundreds of species and hybrids available, many of which are suitable for pot culture. Lilies have always been an integral part of the country house garden; often grown in great stone urns on the terrace, they provided a stunning display for the resident

Lilium 'Casa Blanca'

gentry and their visitors. To emulate this style of planting you should choose lilies which have a soft colour and loose appearance. Unless your containers are in a very sheltered position the long stems of the lilies will need some support. This can be provided by underplanting with shrubby plants like lavender or rosemary which will help support the stems or alternatively you can use twiggy pea sticks which the lilies can grow through, but do be careful not to damage the bulbs when pushing the twigs into the compost.

The dwarf, brightly coloured Asiatic lilies known as patio lilies may have been specially bred for growing in pots, but with their rigid stems and upturned flowers in bright colours they fail to achieve a look of faded splendour.

THE REGAL LILY – *LILIUM REGALE*

Next to the Madonna lily, the regal lily is among the best known and loved of all lilies. The funnel-shaped flowers are white on the inside and flushed with pinkish-purple on the outside. There is a pure white version as well – *L. regale* 'Album'. Each flower is up to 15cm (6in) long and a stem may carry as many as 10 flowers in midsummer. The perfume is very strong and when grown in an unheated greenhouse or conservatory the flowers will fill the air with their delicious scent. Regal lilies need a large container such as a heavy stone-based urn, a wooden half-barrel or a substantial terracotta pot, which will keep the plants stable even when they reach their eventual height of 1.2m (4ft). Pots of lilies can be left outside all winter, but you should protect the young growth from damage by late frosts by spreading fleece over them if a frost is forecast.

THE FLORIST'S LILY – *LILIUM LONGIFLORUM*

Although this lily is not hardy and cannot be left outside all year round, it is well worth potting up some bulbs in winter, ready for putting outside during the summer. This lily produces fewer flowers per stem than the regal lily, but cut-flower enthusiasts love it for the slender pure-white trumpets and wonderful scent. It will reach a height of 1–1.2m (3–4ft).

LILIUM 'MONT BLANC'

A compact cultivar from the Asiatic group of lilies, this one has soft, satiny, creamy-white blooms

---

Growing Lilies

Lilies are best planted in groups of three or five. The bulbs need plenty of rooting space and it is therefore best to avoid pots that are narrow at the base – a straight-sided barrel is far better. With the exception of *L. candidum*, all the lilies mentioned here are stem-rooting, which means they produce feeding roots on the lower part of the stem and need to be planted deeply. Cover the base of the container with drainage material followed by a base layer of loamy compost at least 7.5cm (3in) deep and then a layer of coarse sand on which the bulbs will sit to avoid them rotting in wet winter weather. Set the bulbs 15cm (6in) apart and cover with at least 15cm (6in) of compost.

---

which face upwards, making it a particularly good choice for smaller pots. The stems reach just over 60cm (2ft) in height and produce their blooms from early to midsummer.

LILIUM 'CASA BLANCA'

The most ravishingly beautiful and fragrant of the modern Oriental hybrid lilies, 'Casa Blanca' has

huge, waxy, outward-facing white flowers, each petal richly sprinkled with raised self-coloured dots. The flowers are borne on stems 1.2m (4ft) in height from mid- to late summer. Tubs of 'Casa Blanca' lilies positioned under a bedroom window will fill the night air with their fragrance, which will waft indoors through opened windows.

LILIUM 'PINK PERFECTION'

This is another tall trumpet lily which needs a substantial container. 'Pink Perfection' is a really good faded rose colour which makes a subtle change from the predominantly white lilies mentioned so far. The stems grow to 1.8m (6ft) tall and the striking flowers can measure as much as 15cm (6in) across. As a hybrid it does not possess the strong perfume of either *L. regale* or *L. speciosum*, but the colour is absolutely right for Faded Splendour.

LILIUM SPECIOSUM

Commonly known as the turkscap lily, this species from the Far East has up to 12 nodding pink or white flowers per stem, each petal dotted with pink or crimson dots. It reaches a height of 1.1–1.7m (3$^{1}/_{2}$–5$^{1}/_{2}$ft) and requires a lime-free compost.

Lilium longiflorum

Lilium longiflorum 'Casa Rosa'

Lilium regale

Lilium candidum

'Elizabeth', a scented, repeat-flowering climbing rose such as 'Sombreuil' and fragrant honeysuckle. Spread a layer of gravel on the floor of the greenhouse, position a wooden bench at the end flanked with pots of lilies and you will have created your own little corner of paradise.

Many old-fashioned plants have what is described as a 'lax habit'. This means that they tend to sprawl and intermingle rather than stand to attention. The term also rather appropriately describes the ideal approach to this style of gardening. Don't be too tidy, only mow the grass when strictly necessary, resist staking every plant and find time to relax and enjoy the effect of the plants intermingling. By adopting your own lax habit towards your garden you will find that Faded Splendour becomes easy to achieve.

Nor should you be in a hurry to remedy peeling paintwork or weathered wood. If you must paint, use one of the new ranges of exterior wood stains which come in subtle colours. A soft grey-blue or grey-green would keep the wood in good condition without looking too bright.

It is worth investing in one or two really good, large containers for the Faded Splendour garden – preferably old or one of the very good fibreglass copies which are now available. The fibreglass pots can be nearly as expensive as old pots, but they are more robust and are copies of some of the very finest

Dilapidated sheds and greenhouses are a positive asset when you want to establish a touch of faded splendour in your garden. As long as the structures are safe they can provide a perfect setting for your containers. An old greenhouse with its glass removed looks wonderful with groups of containers planted with flowering plants along its ledges and on its benches. Large pots around the door can be planted with climbers so that the whole building becomes a framework over which the plants can scramble. Even an abandoned old aluminium greenhouse can be transformed into a bower when covered in a canopy of *Clematis montana*

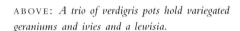

ABOVE: *A trio of verdigris pots hold variegated geraniums and ivies and a lewisia.*

RIGHT: *When you own a jardinière as magnificent as this, the plants are used to show it off rather than the other way round.*

OPPOSITE PAGE: *An old copper with its patina of age is a perfect container for a magnificent datura* (Brugmansia).

antique pots and urns, so they will add grace and dignity to any garden. If expensive pots really are beyond your means there are alternatives which will also conjure up the illusion of a bygone age, but are more 'potting shed' than 'grand terrace'. Old galvanized water tanks, 'dolly' tubs and coppers can all be used as large-scale planters.

In the conservatory and greenhouses of the grand houses of the past wirework hanging baskets, jardinières and plant stands were used to display plants to best advantage. These old pieces have a charm generally lacking in the modern hanging basket, which tends to be made from plastic coated wire. Look out for old ones – they

don't need to be antique to be attractive. Before the advent of plastic coatings most baskets were made from galvanized wire and these now have a nice patina of age. The French have always been enthusiastic manufacturers of decorative wirework and it is still possible to buy relatively inexpensive baskets, plant stands and jardinières of great charm.

Some modern conservatories are very similar in appearance (although on a smaller scale) to those which were built in their Victorian heyday, but virtually all modern conservatories differ from their precursors in one important aspect. The early conservatories were built to accommodate plants first and people second, whereas the reverse is true today, when conservatories are generally viewed as an additional living space for the home. To create the right conditions to replicate the planting style of earlier times your conservatory would need a brick, tile or stone floor, borders edged with decorative bricks for permanent planting of prize specimens, high humidity and good ventilation. None of this is particularly conducive to human comfort.

Obviously some compromise is necessary. If your conservatory is very much a living space with soft furnishings and carpets or rugs you should restrict yourself mainly to houseplants such as *Ficus benjaminii*, *Monstera deliciosa* or *Chamaedorea elegans* which are all very tolerant of the low humidity and variable ventilation in the average conservatory. In the winter you can bring in a few tender plants like pelargoniums or shrubby salvias which don't mind being hot and dry. If you

LEFT: *Heliotropes in a Regency jardinière fill the conservatory with their fragrance.*

ABOVE, RIGHT: *Old terracotta pots and weathered wooden seed trays help set the scene.*

want a room like this to resemble a High Victorian conservatory you will have to rely on the furnishings and bric-a-brac rather than the planting. Rattan blinds, bamboo furniture and ornate china jardinières with dark paintwork would give it period style.

A fortunate few may have an old conservatory or lean-to greenhouse which was built on the old principles and here you will be able to grow many of the plants which delighted the avid collectors last century. This was the age of the plant hunters who travelled the world in search of ever more exotic specimens to offer for sale back home. The arrival of a new plant was a matter of great excitement and people would go to great lengths to obtain a specimen. This was competitive gardening at its most extreme. Today you won't need to find a plant hunter to supply you with unusual tender plants, but you will need to visit nurseries which specialize in the rare and unusual or obtain plants by mail order. Of course some of the plants which were rare then are commonplace now and you will have no difficulty obtaining them – plants like *Jasminum polyanthum* and *Lilium regale*.

Climbing plants can get out of hand in the conservatory, so unless you favour the Miss Havisham style of gardening you will need to cut them back regularly. Jasmine in particular benefits from an annual prune as it only flowers on new growth – stems which

have flowered should be cut back close to the main stem to encourage new shoots. Scented plants are a special pleasure when grown under glass, especially in cooler areas where more tender plants would not thrive out of doors. Recommended scented climbers which are not too rampant are *Hoya carnosa* with its clusters of waxy flowers and its spicy sweet scent, the Chilean jasmine (*Mandevilla laxa*), which has large jasmine-like white flowers, and the incomparable *Stephanotis floribunda*. All three will do best in terracotta pots, planted in a loam-based compost. Topdress annually with slow-release plant food granules and liquid feed during the growing season. These plants need humidity while they are in active growth and will also need some background heat during the winter as they are not frost-hardy.

In the past, generations of trained gardeners worked long hours to keep the houses and conservatories of the gentry filled with flowering plants all year round. That age is long gone, and few of us have the time or inclination to emulate their example, but we can grow the container plants they loved, some as annuals and some which will survive over winter with a minimum of care.

All except the most tender of conservatory plants benefit from being stood outdoors in a sheltered spot during the summer. Conservatories and greenhouses tend to overheat, even with shading, and become breeding grounds for red spider mite, whitefly and scale insect. Moving the plants outdoors allows you an opportunity to give the conservatory a clear out and the plants will enjoy the benefits of direct sun and rain. If you would rather not denude your conservatory of plants you can rotate them so that all have their time outdoors but then return refreshed to decorative duty.

In hot weather you should follow the example of the old gardeners and keep your greenhouse or conservatory cool and humid by watering the paths and floor. As the water evaporates it cools the air and immediately makes the atmosphere plant-friendly. In very hot weather you can do this on your terrace or patio as well if plants begin to droop in the midday sun. Watering the plants themselves could lead to scorching, but

sprinkling the area with water from a watering can will help revive them.

Scented plants are generally the most favoured, and deservedly so as there is another dimension to the pleasure we derive from them. The heliotrope *Heliotropium arborescens* was a great favourite of the Victorians with its delicious vanilla scent and its purple flowers. The variety *H*. 'Marine' has the darkest flowers, but its scent is weak compared with the shrubby varieties such as *H*. 'Chatsworth' and *H*. 'Princess Marina'. If heliotropes are kept in a heated conservatory they will bloom all year round, otherwise they should be cut back by half in late autumn and kept fairly dry in a frost-free place until the spring.

Daturas (*Brugmansia*) are among the most dramatic of conservatory plants, with their huge, fragrant, trumpet-

shaped flowers. The strength of fragrance does vary from one variety to another, *B*. × *candida* and *B. suaveolens* being among the best. Daturas quickly grow into very large plants, so they will need to be planted in a substantial container. They can be stood outside during the summer but slugs and snails find them irresistible, quickly reducing their leaves to lacework, so they will need protection from attack. Daturas are poisonous and there are reports that the scent can be hallucinogenic in confined areas, so these are plants to be treated with respect.

Citrus trees will do well in a conservatory. The most commonly available variety is the Calamondin orange × *Citrofortunella* 'Calamandarin', a small, bushy shrub with fragrant white flowers and small, inedible orange fruit. For edible fruit, Meyer's lemon (*Citrus meyeri* 'Meyer') is best adapted to pot cultivation. (For details of how to care for citrus, see page 16).

The gardenia *Gardenia jasminoides* is another deliciously fragrant shrub with glossy green leaves and pure white flowers. An acid soil is essential and gardenias should be watered with rain water as the lime in tap water can affect them adversely.

There is a temptation to neglect foliage plants in favour of flowers, to think of them as plants of last resort when nothing else will grow, but this is to seriously underrate the impact they can make when grown in containers. A single flowering plant will also draw the eye far more effectively when its flowers are set among attractive foliage plants than when it is vying for attention alongside other flowers.

Certainly foliage plants were the backbone of the display in the conservatories of the past, where asparagus fern (*Asparagus densiflorus*), palms and ferns provided a year-round backdrop for seasonal plants. *Coleus* with their multi-coloured leaves were hugely popular as conservatory plants and were grown outdoors in pots and borders during the summer. After years of disdain they are popular once more and are entirely appropriate for

the Faded Splendour garden, especially if you avoid the temptation of planting too many colour variants in just one container.

Mother-in-law's-tongue (*Sansevieria trifasciata*), the Swiss cheese plant (*Monstera deliciosa*), the maranta (*Maranta leuconeuro*) and especially the aspidistra (*Aspidistra elatior*) are all plants with a bit of an image problem as they are mostly frequently seen barely surviving and covered in dust in some unsuitable

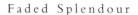

LEFT: *The informal planting is perfect for this magnificent old stone trough.*

RIGHT: *Topiary box and ornamental cabbages in antique terracotta pots have a delightfully formal appearance.*

position on a windowsill or in a dark hallway. Given a bit of love and attention in a frost-free conservatory or greenhouse, they make splendid evergreen container plants.

Box (*Buxus*) and ivy (*Hedera*) have long been important container plants and their dense growth and evergreen foliage make them ideal subjects for training into topiary shapes. Both plants are very hardy, undemanding and pretty well pest- and disease-free, especially if

planted in a loam-based compost and top dressed annually with slow-release plant food granules. Common box (*Buxus sempervirens*) is ideal for training into balls, cubes and pyramids or even something more ambitious if you have the eye for it. For the less adventurous, garden centres now sell frames which can be fitted round the growing plant and as the branches protrude beyond the frame they can be trimmed to shape. Contrary to what you may think, it doesn't take more than two to three years to train a young box plant into a reasonable shape, especially if it is watered regularly and given a liquid feed during the growing season.

Buying ready-made topiary can be an expensive business, but if you consider even two to three years too long to wait you may prefer to train ivy into topiary shapes instead. There are lots of different wire frames you can choose from, from the classical ball or cone to the whimsical – bird, cat or rabbit. For the Faded Splendour garden the traditional shapes would be more appropriate. A huge range of ivies is available, but you should resist the temptation to buy large-leaved, fast-growing varieties which would soon swamp the frame and conceal its shape. The smaller the leaf the more defined

will be the outline, but some of the very small-leaved ivies are rather slow-growing for this purpose. There are so many different cultivars available that rather than recommending a specific variety the best advice is to buy the most readily available which are sold as house or container plants. Repot the plant into a loam-based compost to avoid problems with vine weevil and push the frame into place. Separate the stems and twist them individually around the frame. Water regularly and give a liquid feed every fortnight throughout the growing season. Keep twisting the new growth around the frame and trim off leaves which spoil the outline.

Farmyard

Country people have always turned to the farmyard for their containers and everything from a cattle manger to a bucket with a hole in it can be given a second lease of life when planted with flowers of the countryside such as buttercups and daisies.

FARMYARD STYLE IS very much a romanticized version of the reality, which is often more utilitarian than decorative. In truth, few of us would want our garden to resemble a working farmyard with the seasonal mud or dust, the machinery, the patches of weeds and the smells; but there are elements within the whole picture which are both charming and decorative and which can be interpreted in container planting.

Farmyard-inspired style makes use of recycled agricultural items – troughs, mangers, feeders and hoppers from the animal pens, pitchers, buckets, churns and pails from the dairy and weathered timber and chicken wire from the barn. With modern farming practices many of these are no longer used, and certainly anything in a state of disrepair will be discarded rather than mended. Some will make ideal planters for a farmyard-style garden, especially when the theme is further emphasized by the inclusion of old tools as decorative objects. You can also evoke the farmyard by using utilitarian materials like chicken wire, tin and aluminium which are cheap, light and easily shaped to make containers.

This style of garden will be more appropriate and easier to achieve if you live in a fairly rural location or in a town surrounded by countryside rather than in the city, where it could look rather out of place and the containers could be difficult to locate and certainly expensive to buy.

Flowers should be simple and unpretentious. Accentuate the theme by including native plants which, although decorative, are generally thought of as weeds, such as the ox-eye daisy (*Leucanthemum vulgare*), feverfew (*Tanacetum parthenium*) and buttercups (*Ranunculus acris*). Add other flowers in the cream and buttery-yellow country colours – dwarf potentillas, rock roses (*Helianthemum*), yellow and cream ox-eye chamomile (*Anthemis tinctoria*), and for spring small wild daffodils (*Narcissus pseudonarcissus*), cowslips (*Primula veris*) and primroses (*Primula vulgaris*). Many of these plants were once cultivated in farmyards for use in country remedies for a variety of ailments.

LEFT: *A yellow marguerite looks very like a buttercup but will flower for a longer period.*

RIGHT: *A summer meadow basket overflows with yellow and white marguerites, double-flowered chamomile and ox-eye daisies.*

Craft Project 8

CHICKEN WIRE WINDOW BOX

YOU WILL NEED

• 38mm × 19mm (1½in × ¾in)
rough timber battens cut to
the following lengths:
6 lengths 600mm (24in) long
4 lengths 100mm (4in) long
4 lengths 150mm (6in) long
• Medium-gauge chicken wire
• 8 × 75mm (3in) and 8 ×
50mm (2in) woodscrews
• 8 × 25mm (1in) nails
• Electric or hand drill
• Screwdriver
• Heavy-duty staple gun
and staples
• Hammer
• Hand saw
• Tin snips or old scissors
• Heavy-duty gloves (for
protection when cutting
netting)

SIMPLE ROUGH timber
battens and chicken wire
are all you need for this basic
farmyard-style window box,
which can even be made by
those with only rudimentary
carpentry skills.

Construction

1. Assemble the front and
back of the window box.
Each requires two 600mm
(24in) lengths and two
100mm (4in) lengths. Drill
clearance and pilot holes
then screw together using
75mm (3in) screws.
2. Join the front and back of
the window box, using four
150mm (6in) lengths of
timber to make the side
struts. Drill all four corners
of the front and back (as

before) then screw together
using 50mm (2in) screws.
3. Position the last two
600mm (24in) lengths of
batten across the bottom of
the window box to form the
slatted base. Nail in position
with 25mm (1in) nails.
4. If you wish to paint the
window box this is the best
time to do it unless you want
to paint the wire as well.
Once the paint is dry staple
the wire netting to the front,
base, back and sides of the
window box, folding over all
the sharp cut ends. The
front, base and back can use
a continuous length of
chicken wire, doubled over
for a more dense effect. Cut
separate panels for the sides
and staple in place.

TO DECORATE

• Red oxide paint
• Paintbrush

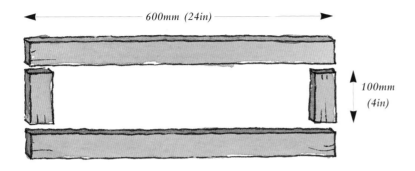

600mm (24in)

100mm (4in)

1. Assemble the front panel and screw together with 75mm (3in) screws. Repeat for back panel.

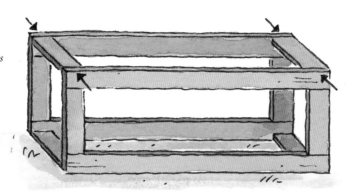

2. Join the front and back panels together using four 150mm (6in) lengths of timber as side struts and screw together with 50mm (2in) screws.

3. Nail the base slats in position.

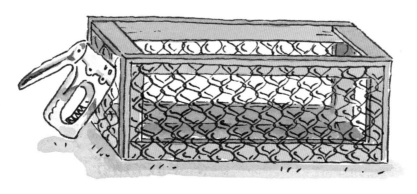

4. Cover the front, back, sides and base with a double layer of chicken wire and staple in place.

ChickenWire

Chicken wire comes in various gauges which determine the size of the holes in the netting. If you already have a roll or a short length it can be used for this project whatever the gauge.

Variations

Although the chicken wire looks great on the window box, it really isn't worth buying a whole roll just for this project. As an alternative you could nail vertical strips of batten around the window box to give it a slatted appearance. If each slat is given a pointed top the end result will resemble a miniature picket fence.

Plant Profile

BUTTERCUPS AND DAISIES

*Wild buttercups and daisies are usually the flowers that first
come to mind when people think of meadows. However, their
fragile charm can be lost in a small-scale planting and it is
sometimes better to choose a showier variety.*

Just the idea of a garden full of buttercups and daisies conjures up nostalgic images of childhood walks by a stream and afternoons spent lazing in a flowery meadow. Yet many of the buttercups and daisies which we now cultivate in our gardens are a long way from the ones we remember, bearing little resemblance to the simple floret rays of the white daisies which we gathered to make necklaces or the dainty yellow buttercups we used to wave under our chins. As time has moved on the plant breeders have stepped in and provided us with a vast array of multi-coloured flowers which

Chrysogonum virginianum

still come under the banner of 'daisy' or 'buttercup'.

Yet all is not lost – there are still members of the Compositae and Ranunculaceae families which retain the spirit of the originals. The plants selected here stay within the original colour spectrum, ranging from pure white through cream to deepest yellow, and will give your farmyard containers an air of informality and originality.

BUTTERCUPS
RANUNCULUS ASIATICUS

The Asian buttercup behaves more like an alpine (which it is) than a true buttercup. For a start it likes a sun-baked position and is not always hardy, which makes it a good candidate for containers which can be moved to a frost-free position for the winter. In appearance it resembles a poppy or windflower with slender branching stems and open-faced

flowers. Choose the single-colour varieties in white or yellow rather than the mixtures, which contain a high proportion of oranges and reds. The compost it is grown in should be a free-draining loam mixture with added coarse grit.

RANUNCULUS GRAMINEUS

Another alpine from the buttercup family, *R. gramineus* forms clumps 40cm (16in) high by 15cm (6in) across of grass-like blue foliage bearing loose sprays of bright yellow flowers from late spring to early summer. Like *R. asiaticus* it likes a sunny or partially shaded position and well-drained compost.

Ranunculus asiaticus 'Mount Hermon'

Ranunculus asiaticus

Argyranthemum foeniculaceum

Both species can be increased by dividing the plants after flowering.

CALTHA PALUSTRIS

The marsh marigold is also one of the buttercup family, but the conditions it prefers are very different. This is a marginal plant and it will do well on a shallow ledge in a water-filled container or in one which is being used as a miniature bog garden. The bright golden-yellow flowers are borne in mid to late spring, and although the flowering season is short they are worth including for the purity and intensity of their colour. The double form 'Flore Plena' is also very attractive but lacks the simple beauty of the single flowers.

DAISIES
ARGYRANTHEMUM

A. frutescens is one of the best-known and most stylish members of the daisy family. Traditionally grown as a standard, it can be seen in all the most fashionable town gardens. Nevertheless, with its light, feathery foliage and abundant,

classic daisy flowers with their yellow centres and perfect halo of pure white petals its simplicity is quite appropriate for a farmyard scheme. Whether trained as a standard or not, *A. frutescens* can reach a height of 90cm (3ft) and makes an ideal subject for a large container. A plant can be kept for two to three years, but after that it tends to become leggy and lose vigour. Take cuttings in late summer. It needs frost protection in all but the mildest and most sheltered of gardens.

A. foeniculaceum is a close relation but with finer, bluey-green foliage, while *A. gracile* 'Chelsea Girl' has unusual silvery, filigree foliage which beautifully sets off the single white flowers.

Two of the best yellow argyranthemums are *A.* 'Jamaica Primrose' and *A. maderense* pale form. 'Jamaica Primrose' has

Argyranthemum frutescens

buttercup-yellow flowers and fresh green foliage, while *A. maderense* has charming soft yellow flowers with blue-green foliage.

LEUCANTHEMUM

A smaller group of daisies, but with the same typical flower formation is found in the *Leucanthemum* genus (formerly *Chrysanthemum*). The marguerite or ox-eye daisy (*Leucanthemum vulgare*) is a native of many parts of the northern hemisphere and can be grown in containers where it will reach a height and spread of 60cm × 30cm (24in × 12in). It is a hardy perennial, easy to grow in multi-purpose compost, and produces flowers from late spring to early summer.

Smaller still is the alpine *Leucanthemum alpinum* or moon daisy, a compact plant ideal for sink gardens or alpine pots. It

Leucanthemum vulgare

prefers a loam-based compost with one-third added grit and will benefit from a topdressing of gravel. It likes an open, sunny position, where it will be hardy and generally evergreen. It will reach a height of 15cm (6 in) with a spread of 25cm (10in).

CHRYSOGONUM
VIRGINIANUM

The golden star, as it is commonly known, is a native of the eastern USA and has one of the longest flowering periods of the summer perennials – right through from late spring until autumn. Although neither a buttercup nor a daisy, it has some similarities and mixes well with them. The small golden-yellow, star-shaped flowers appear on a compact plant with bright green leaves which are semi-evergreen. It likes a moist compost and can be positioned in sun or partial shade. It is a good choice for a basket or small container, reaching a height of 20cm (8in) with a 30cm (12in) spread.

The starting point for a garden with a farmyard theme may be nostalgia for the holidays of your childhood, a style decision or even a practical solution for what to do with a shed full of agricultural scrap, but wherever you start you will need to set the scene or your farmyard containers could look uncomfortable in their surroundings. For instance, an old milk churn overflowing with yellow and white daisies accompanied by a galvanized pail tumbling with yellow stonecrop (*Sedum acre*) looks great against a weathered brick wall, but the same container planted with pelargoniums, lobelia and alyssum, standing on modern paving slabs against a wooden fence panel, looks contrived and inappropriate.

Farmyard style is not really suitable for a new garden, nor does it sit comfortably in an urban environment, but it can look good in any established country garden. Many rural houses still have outbuildings with their own small paved yards which in the past were used to house a cow, a pig or some chickens. This sort of enclosed area would be ideal for a farmyard-style garden with an old iron hay rack as a planted wall basket and various metal and wooden containers filled with simple country flowers arranged around the yard.

It isn't necessary to give the entire garden over to a farmyard theme – a single item such as an old cartwheel propped against a stone wall or a wooden wheelbarrow can create a focal point around which you can create a subtle display which uses old agricultural containers and implements as decoration. Planted with a mixture of cottage-garden plants, wildflowers and grasses, your farmyard containers will be both charming and unusual.

If you live in the country, farm sales and agricultural markets can be a source of farmyard containers – although with the former you may find that you have to buy several items in a lot in order to obtain the one thing that you are after. In general, country junk shops, reclamation yards and boot sales are a better bet. Even here some of the more decorative items such as milk churns, cattle troughs and old mangers now fetch high prices, so you may need to focus on more mundane objects such as galvanized pails, tin baths, old sieves and heavy iron pots and troughs which have been used as feed or water containers for livestock.

Once you have a few authentic bits and pieces you can supplement these by making or customizing some of your own containers. As an example, chicken wire is a particularly versatile material and can easily be worked into alternatives to the ubiquitous hanging basket, or even used to disguise a basket by covering its exterior surface with moss and then wrapping it in two or three layers of chicken wire.

RIGHT: *Brightly coloured dahliettas in miniature galvanized buckets look just right in the chicken-wire window box.*

ABOVE: *An outbuilding is dressed for a party with farmyard relics, straw bales and buckets of flowers.*

On the whole farmers are practical people without the time or inclination to do more than is strictly necessary when it comes to decoration; painting is done to preserve rather than embellish, and the choice of colours is guided by what tins of paint can be found in the barn or which colours are on a cheap offer at the local hardware store rather than by a lengthy process of pouring over a colour chart. The palette is generally fairly limited – black, white, cream, brown and green, with red oxide and aluminium paint used on metalwork.

Although red oxide is really a primer for metal it is a great colour which can be hard to match in other types of paint, so if you can't find a suitable alternative you can use it on wood as well. Stick to a single colour for each container – fancy paint finishes play no part in farmyard style.

Because of its durability and low maintenance, galvanized metal has always been popular on farms. Buckets, troughs, water tanks, watering cans and

baths are still made in this material and old ones are quite easy to get hold of. Old doesn't have to mean antique – after a couple of years galvanized metal loses its shiny new appearance and develops a soft bloom which tones it down to a muted matt grey. These can all be used as containers, although in most instances you will probably need to drill drainage holes in the base using a drill bit suitable for metal.

When most non-farmers picture a farmyard the image conjured up is usually one of gentle decay and benign neglect – weathered wood, peeling

ABOVE: *An old sieve makes an ideal container for succulents, which do best in very free-draining soil.*

paintwork and decoratively rusting metal, with drifts of daisies, buttercups and dandelions, a lost Arcadia which needs only occasional human intervention to maintain its perfection. Such a farmyard would be anathema to a working farmer, but it is perfectly acceptable as a vision on which to base a farmyard-style garden. This is not a style for the very tidy gardener – it is at its most successful when things are left to settle into their surroundings, when containers as well as the plants appear to have taken root and flowers self-seed and spread around the garden.

Ideally, walls should be weathered brick or stone as they make a more sympathetic background than a painted wall or fence, although both of the latter can be improved. A painted wall can be used as a display area for old farm tools and a wooden fence will benefit from a coat of black wood stain. York stone, brick or cobbles are the best type of paving for this style of garden as they all improve with age and plants will quickly colonize their crevices.

In the farmyard garden old tools are not arranged but are rather left where they were last used – not on the whole good gardening practice, but fine when the tools are already rusted and have outlived their useful life. Garden sieves can be hung from nails on walls and an old wooden field gate which has long since been replaced by a lighter, more durable metal one can be propped against a wall where climbing plants can scramble up and through it. This is a relaxed style of gardening where nature should be allowed to exert her influence.

There was a time not long ago when we were in danger of losing many of our wild flowers through over-enthusiastic use of herbicides and fertilizers, not just on farms but also in parks, on roadside verges and in allotments and gardens. Thankfully we are beginning to understand the damage that these sprays can do, not just to flowers but to the whole natural ecology, and many farmers, local authorities and gardeners are now taking a more gentle approach. As a result the countryside has begun to bloom again and we can enjoy the pleasure of verges carpeted with flowers in spring and summer, of fields of corn red with poppies and parks where areas of grass are left to grow long, allowing bulbs and flowers to seed and multiply. The fact that some of these flowers have regenerated from the brink of extinction is a tribute to their resilience and their undemanding nature.

Growing wildflowers in containers is not difficult – in most cases they need little attention once established, so if you are a gardener who constantly tidies and trims your plants you may even find them too low-maintenance for your liking. It is also true that most varieties of wildflowers bloom from early spring to midsummer, after which the garden can look rather dull, but if you are someone who goes away in the summer this can be a positive benefit – while you are sunning yourself on the beach, the wildflowers are ripening and setting

seed and will survive all but the hottest weather without water.

Creating the right conditions to grow wildflowers is as much a matter of observation as anything else – see where they grow in the wild and you will know whether they are likely to grow successfully in your garden. Primroses (*Primula vulgaris*), violets (*Viola riviniana*), comfrey (*Symphytum officinale*), forget-me-not (*Myosotis arvensis*), mint (*Mentha spicata*), the various members of the deadnettle family (*Lamium*), bluebell (*Hyacinthoides non-scripta*) and foxglove (*Digitalis purpurea*) will all do well in containers in a damp, shady garden, while the field flowers such as the poppy (*Papaver rhoeas*), cornflower (*Centaurea cyanus*) and ox-eye daisy (*Leucanthemum vulgare*) and sun-loving plants such as creeping thymes (*Thymus serpyllum*), harebell (*Campanula rotundifolia*) and maiden pink (*Dianthus deltoides*) all need an open sunny position. For shade-loving plants use a mixture of 2 parts multi-purpose compost, 2 parts loam-based compost such as John Innes No. 2 and 1 part composted bark or leafmould. Sun-loving plants need a loam-based compost with added grit to ensure good drainage. Peat-based composts are not suitable for growing wildflowers in containers.

Most garden centres now sell packets of wildflower seeds and collections of wildflower plants which have been produced by licensed growers. You should resist the temptation to collect

from the wild, even where plants are plentiful, as this has contributed to the scarcity of many plants which once were commonplace. Fifty years ago

cowslips (*Primula veris*) carpeted every meadow in springtime and they were picked by the armful; now they are more common on railway embankments and motorway verges than they are on farms. Not only is it irresponsible to pick wild flowers, in many cases it is now also illegal.

ABOVE: *An old wooden wheelbarrow is filled with wildflowers. The poppies and cornflowers need little attention while they grow, and if they are left to self-seed you can expect a repeat performance next year.*

I n the past every farmyard had its
pond – a source of water for the
livestock and the garden and home
to the resident ducks and geese. Rushes,
flag iris (*Iris pseudoacorus*), marsh
marigolds (*Caltha palustris*) and water
forget-me-not (*Myosotis scorpioides*)
lined its boggy margins, making it
picturesque as well as functional.

It is surprisingly easy to make a pond
or bog garden out of an old trough,
water tank or large pot, and you will
need neither running water nor an
electric pump to do so. For a pond you
will need a fairly large container which
should be more or less as deep as it is
wide. This will allow you to plant
oxygenators in the deep water to create
a natural healthy balance. Specialist
water-garden nurseries will have a good
selection of oxygenators, water lilies and
marginal plants and the labels will give
clear instructions on the depth of water
preferred by each plant. This type of
pond is also ideal for some of the
smaller varieties of water lily, as they
hate to be planted in moving water.
Marginal plants such as marsh marigolds,
water forget-me-nots and sweet flag
(*Acorus calamus* 'Variegatus') will need to
be provided with a ledge in shallow
water. The easiest way to do this is to
stack bricks to one side of the container
and rest a slate or slab of stone on top
of the bricks before filling the pond
with water.

Cover the bottom of the container
with at least 10cm (4in) of washed

LEFT: *Old cast-iron pig troughs have been used as miniature bog gardens for marginal plants.*

RIGHT: *Marsh marigolds, cowslips and golden-leaved feverfew nestle in a bed of straw in an old galvanized bucket.*

gravel, which will help keep the water clear as any soil from the plants can sink below the gravel where it will not be disturbed. All the plants will do best planted in aquatic baskets (plastic baskets with finely slatted sides) lined with hessian and filled with ordinary garden soil or aquatic compost. The usual types of potting compost are not suitable as they contain too much nitrogen.

Position your container so that it is in full sun for at least part of the day – water lilies in particular need sun to flower well. It will take a couple of months for the pond to settle down, but after that you should have few problems with the possible exception of blanket weed, which may form in the water. The easiest way to remove this is to place a cane in the centre of the mass and twist it – the weed will wrap around the cane and can be lifted out.

If marginal plants are your passion you might consider a bog garden instead of a pond. A bog garden creates the conditions that exist at the edge of a pond – shallow water and mud. You can use any fairly shallow container with a watertight base for this purpose. Drill holes in the container about halfway up the sides so that the plants can have their lower roots in the water but will not become waterlogged. Bog gardens can become smelly, but this can be controlled by spreading a layer of charcoal across the bottom of the container before filling it with gravel and then plunging the plants in the gravel. The candelabra group of primulas including *Primula helodoxa*, *P. bulleyana* and *P.* 'Inverewe' are all beautiful plants for a bog garden, as are members of the mimulus family and the stunning red *Lobelia cardinalis*.

In the past the role of the farmer's wife was far more than that of cook, housekeeper and mother. She was the home apothecary, in charge of the stillroom where she brewed ale, made wines and cordials, dried and preserved medicinal and aromatic plants and generally ensured the health and well-being of her family. She grew some of the plants which she used in her lotions and potions in pots on her windowsills, some in containers grouped around the stillroom door and others in the kitchen garden, supplementing them with those she gathered from the surrounding hedgerows and fields. These home-made country remedies were the most commonly used and most effective medicines of their day. Doctors of the time killed as often as they cured with medical advice based more on a mixture of superstition, ignorance and arrogance than science.

Modern scientists are exploring the effectiveness of many of these old-fashioned remedies and it is quite extraordinary how often their findings confirm the traditional use of a particular plant. If the medicinal use of plants interests you, you could create your own natural pharmacy by planting your farmyard-style containers with a selection of the herbs and other plants which can be used for simple home cures, herbal teas and tisanes. Many of the plants are also culinary herbs which we use every day in our cooking, but we don't always think of them in their other roles as healing and soothing remedies.

Most of us think of sage (*Salvia officinalis*) as a herb to be used in stuffings, but it has long had a reputation for healing, the name salvia itself being derived from the Latin word salvere, meaning 'to save'. The herbalist Gerard said that it was effective at restoring the memory and recent research suggests this may be correct, so a plant or two of sage should definitely be included in your natural pharmacy. Sage needs to be planted in a loam-based compost with added grit and should stand in a sunny position. An infusion of purple sage (*Salvia officinalis* 'Purpurascens') and honey is also a traditional cold and cough cure.

Peppermint (*Mentha × piperita*) has never lost popularity as a herbal tea to be taken to aid digestion. Plant it in a moisture-retentive soil in a large pot or an old tin bucket with a hole in the bottom and put it in a shady part of the garden. It is a greedy plant which needs topdressing with compost to keep it productive. The flowers of chamomile (*Chamaemelum nobile*) are a gentle sedative when taken as a tea at bedtime. Plant it in full sun in free-draining soil. Lemon verbena (*Aloysia triphylla* syn. *Lippia citriodora*) is a wonderfully fragrant lemon-scented shrub. The leaves make a delicious tea which helps digestion and settles the stomach. It is a tender shrub which will need protecting from frost. Feverfew (*Tanacetum parthenium*) is a pretty plant with white daisy flowers and yellow-green leaves which will do well in full sun. Traditionally it was

planted around a house to purify the air and ward off disease and, as its name indicates, was much used to dispel fever. More recently it has become popular as

an alternative treatment for migraine – the leaves are put into a sandwich and eaten. You should check with your doctor before trying this.

Home-grown chamomile flowers (LEFT) can be picked and used to make a gently sedative herbal tea, while feverfew (RIGHT) has been used as a cure for migraine.

The picturesque old farmyards with hollyhocks round the door and chickens scratching in the yard are seldom part of a modern working farm, but they are still part of smallholding life. Many smallholders are people who have rejected urban life and moved to the country to fulfil a dream, and their gardens reflect this with a mixture of pretty and practical plants which would look delightful in containers with a farmyard theme.

Hollyhocks (*Alcea rosea*) were traditionally planted against the walls of the house because they helped draw moisture from the walls – an important function in the days before damp-proof courses. Surprisingly for a plant their size they will grow well in a container, preferably a fairly large one, although they can grow in very confined spaces. Hollyhocks are easily grown from seed, and once established will self-seed freely.

Scented climbers and old-fashioned roses can cluster round the front door, just as they do in a traditional cottage garden. A deep trough or old water tank will hold two or three climbing plants which can be trained up walls and around a doorway. A variety of the sweetly scented honeysuckle *Lonicera periclymenum* such as 'Serotina' or 'Graham Thomas' planted with *Jasminum polyanthum* and a fragrant rose such as 'Albertine' or 'Mme Alfred Carrière' will make rapid growth if planted in good soil and topdressed regularly with compost. Clustered around the large container, pots of lilies, pinks, lavender and catmint will add further colour and fragrance to a pretty entrance.

The plants that are grown around the kitchen door are usually more functional. This is an ideal spot for the herbs which are used most frequently, and for other edible plants which are decorative as well as tasty. A pair of standard gooseberry bushes placed either side of the kitchen door would be perfect for this style of garden. Although not as easy to obtain as ordinary gooseberry bushes, they are becoming more popular and a good garden centre should be able to order them for you. Rhubarb will do well in a half tub stood in partial shade. Plant it in very rich compost with plenty of added manure, and wait until the second year before picking any stems to allow the plant to establish. A strawberry pot filled with a mixture of regular and alpine strawberries will allow you to pick strawberries over a long period.

Be sure to have pots of mint, thyme, rosemary and parsley near at hand. Although herbs can be planted together in a container you do need to separate them into the Mediterranean herbs which enjoy hot, dry conditions and the shade-loving herbs which need cool, moist conditions. Rosemary and thyme belong to the former category and mint and parsley to the latter. Sorrel has always been a popular herb/vegetable in the country as it was believed to purify the blood. Nowadays it is more valued for its culinary pleasures, and a pot will provide you with tender green leaves to

use in sauces and soups. Among the fruit and herbs, plant edible flowers such as pot marigolds (*Calendula officinalis*), pansies and nasturtiums for inclusion in colourful salads and you too will be able to enjoy the pleasures of the smallholders' garden which aims to please both the eye and the palate.

ABOVE: *Old buckets are home to a selection of edible plants including rhubarb, chard, sorrel, Welsh onions and leeks, all of which look very decorative even when they go to seed.*

Kitchen Garden

The pleasure of eating home-grown

fruit and vegetables is an experience

not to be missed and with modern

compact varieties it is possible to

container-grow many of your favourites.

A mixture of ornamental vegetables

and flowers will ensure your containers

are pretty as well as practical.

THE KITCHEN GARDEN is synonymous with country living. It is hard to imagine a country garden without a vegetable plot, a few fruit trees and a herb or salad bed, often sited near the house, so that fresh produce is always on hand.

The primary function of the kitchen garden has always been to provide the family with fresh, home-grown food for as much of the year as possible, but many have a charm which is way beyond the functional – the most appealing English cottage gardens and French potagers are those where flowers and edible plants jostle for space. Runner beans and sweet peas scramble up bean poles, sunflowers tower above courgette plants, and nasturtiums twine through lettuces and other salad plants, creating a little Eden to make all of us hunger for the rural idyll.

The Kitchen Garden theme is eminently adaptable and equally suitable for a small town garden or a more spacious country garden. The planting can be very informal, with the main effect being one of luxurious abundance, or it can be more formal with vegetables planted in geometric patterns where their colour and form create designs inspired by those in the potager at the Château de Villandry in the Loire Valley.

The basic prerequisites for a kitchen garden are a sunny situation and an eye for containers which complement the theme. Green and white enamelware, discarded cooking pots, weathered terracotta and old wooden barrels can be grouped together ready for planting with a medley of fruit, flowers and vegetables. Old wheelbarrows and even wooden vegetable boxes can be given a coat of paint and become part of the homely scene. Most of the vegetables and herbs can be grown easily from seed or bought as young plants in the spring. Some, for example globe artichokes, will need to be nurtured through the winter but will reward you with magnificent foliage and delicious eating for years to come, while others, such as tomatoes and salad crops, are discarded at the end of the season and renewed each year.

LEFT: *Planting violas among the culinary herbs in these containers gives them a more decorative appearance.*

RIGHT: *One way to create a stunning effect is to fill a container with a single variety of plant, such as this barrel planted with fennel.*

Craft Project 9

BASIL BOXES

YOU WILL NEED

- 18mm (¾in) thick timber
for front, back, sides, base, and
4 feet 90mm × 50mm
(3½in × 2in)
- 32mm (1¼in) thick timber
for handle assembly
- 40mm (1½in) nails
- 4 × 25mm (1in) woodscrews
- 2 × 75mm (3in) woodscrews
- Electric or hand saw
- Screwdriver
- Hammer
- Electric or hand drill
- Spokeshave (optional)
- Vice (optional)
- Medium-grade sandpaper

A TRUG-STYLE planter is a perfect container for basil which can be stood in the sunniest spot in the garden and carried into the kitchen when needed. This project is suitable for anyone with basic experience of carpentry.

Construction

1. Cut out the front, back, two sides, base and feet from 18mm (¾in) thick timber (see opposite). Drill drainage holes in the base panel.
2. Cut the top and side pieces of the handle from 38mm (1½in) thick timber (see opposite). Experienced carpenters can shape a grip by fixing the top piece in a vice and using a spokeshave.
3. Join the front and side panels, using 40mm (1½in) nails. Repeat the process to join the back panel to the side panels.
4. Turn the box upside down and nail the base into position. Nail the feet of the box in place at each corner.
5. Mark the position of the handle uprights halfway along the front and back panels. Screw each upright in place, using two 25mm (1in) screws, then screw the handle grip in place using 75mm (3in) screws.
6. Rub down all the surfaces with sandpaper. Paint the box inside and out with paint or wood stain.

TO DECORATE

- Satin finish paint or water-based preservative wood stain
- Paintbrush

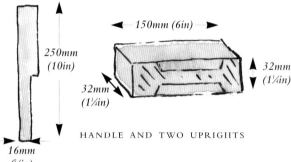

400mm (16in)

350mm (14in)

175mm (7in)

FRONT AND BACK

140mm (5½in)

TWO SIDES

350mm (14in)

175mm (7in)

BASE

250mm (10in)

16mm (⅝in)

150mm (6in)

32mm (1¼in)

32mm (1¼in)

HANDLE AND TWO UPRIGHTS

1. Nail the front panel to the side panels using 40mm (1½in) nails. Repeat with the back panel.

2. Turn the box upside down and nail the base into position. Nail the feet in place at each corner.

3. Screw the handle uprights in position using 25mm (1in) screws.

4. Slot the handle between the uprights and screw in place using 75mm (3in) screws.

A Basic Handle

The box itself is very easy to make; it is the handle which requires a bit more skill. You can make a much simpler handle with a short length of rope. Drill holes large enough to feed the rope through on either side of the box. Thread the rope through the holes from the outside and knot firmly on the inside. Because this type of handle moves, the box is not as stable as it would be with a fixed handle, but it is perfectly adequate when carried with a steadying hand.

ORNAMENTAL VEGETABLES

In containers, where space is inevitably limited, you should grow only plants which are good-looking as well as good to eat. There are plenty of varieties to choose from and when they are accompanied by edible flowers you will find that your garden doesn't have to sacrifice looks for flavour.

As gardens have become smaller it has become much more acceptable and even fashionable to mix the planting of fruit, vegetables and flowers. While most kitchen gardens of the past featured some flowers, it was thought to be somewhat eccentric to plant fruit and vegetables in the flower garden. Nowadays oak-leaf lettuces nestle among love-in-a-mist and delphiniums and ruby chard brings colour and drama to the summer border. Many of these plants will grow happily in containers, where each can be individually cosseted to produce an abundant crop.

GLOBE ARTICHOKE

The globe artichoke is a wonderfully architectural plant with silver-grey serrated leaves and magnificent blue thistle-like flowers. The edible part of the plant is the immature flowerhead, which is best picked while still in tight bud. Artichokes are best bought as named variety young plants, preferably from a nursery which specializes in culinary plants, as the plants at your local garden centre could well be more

Globe artichoke

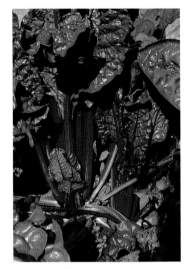

Rhubarb chard

Courgette 'Zucchini'

Runner bean 'Pickwick'

ornamental than edible. Each artichoke will need to be planted in a large container such as a half-barrel in a rich compost with plenty of added manure. If well-fed and watered it will produce a crop of small artichokes in the autumn of the first year, and will then produce a summer crop of full-sized artichokes for the next two years. Although plants can live for six years they weaken progressively after the third year and are best discarded, but not before you have detached rooted suckers from around the crown which will provide you with your replacement plants. Globe artichokes are not fully hardy, so in the autumn trim the foliage to about 45cm (18in) and give the plant a protective covering of straw or fleece.

RHUBARB CHARD (ALSO KNOWN AS RUBY CHARD)

This is a highly ornamental and heavy-cropping biennial spinach with bright red leaf ribs and red-veined, dark-green leaves. Sow seeds thinly directly into the

Cherry tomato 'Sweet 100'

Lettuce 'Red Salad Bowl'

Lettuce 'Green Salad Bowl'

Bean 'Blue lake white seeded'

container in April and thin the seedlings to 20cm (8in) apart. Always pick the leaves as soon as they mature to encourage the formation of more foliage. Chard will crop heavily all summer, slow down through the autumn and winter and then produce a further flush of young growth in the early spring before finally going to seed. Keep an eye out for slug and snail damage.

COURGETTES

Courgette are very productive and attractive container plants. Planted in an old tin bath in very rich compost with lots of added manure, they will grow at an astonishing rate in warm weather provided they are never allowed to dry out and are given regular liquid feeds. Pick the courgettes regularly to keep the plants producing more fruit – left on the plant they will quickly assume the proportions of a marrow and suck all the energy out of the plant. Yellow-fruited

varieties are particularly decorative and still taste good.

TOMATOES

Most of us have tried to grow tomatoes with varying degrees of success. Don't be put off if you have failed previously, as some of the modern cherry tomato varieties have been bred especially for containers and will crop heavily for months, even in poor weather. There was a time when you would have to grow your tomato plants from seed if you wanted to be certain of good flavour, but nowadays garden centres are much better at supplying a good selection of varieties – look out for 'Tumbler', which has been specially bred for hanging baskets, while Sweet 100 is a heavy-cropping cherry tomato and 'Santa' is a miniature plum tomato with deep red fruit and delicious flavour. Position your tomato plants in the sunniest part of the garden, planted in a rich, free-draining

compost, and give them weekly liquid feeds.

LETTUCES

The best way to grow lettuce is to sow a few seeds in a small pot once a fortnight during spring and early summer and then transplant the seedlings into their final position. This way you will have a succession of lettuce rather than a glut. Wooden fruit and vegetable trays from the greengrocer make ideal miniature beds for this type of planting. Line the boxes with a layer of straw, fill with a standard potting compost and transplant the small lettuce seedlings 15cm (6in) apart. Water regularly. 'Little Gem' is always sweet, delicious and reliable and looks good grown alongside the Italian 'Lollo Rosso' and a compact butterhead such as 'Tom Thumb'. Alternatively you could try one of the 'salad bowl' or 'oak-leaf' lettuces, which produce a mass of frilly-edged leaves which can be picked from

the plant as required while the plant continues to grow and produce more leaves.

BEANS

Climbing beans and dwarf beans will grow successfully and attractively in containers. Both need a deep, fertile soil with plenty of well-rotted compost or manure. A tub or half-barrel is an ideal container. There are two types of climbing beans – runner beans and French beans. Runner beans are a traditional cottage-garden favourite and will crop heavily in good weather, while French beans are more reliable in poor weather as they don't need to be pollinated by bees. Both will need poles or canes to climb up, while the dwarf varieties of runner beans and French beans grow on bushes rather than climbing plants. Interplant runner beans with sweet peas (*Lathryus odoratus*) for improved pollination and sweetly scented flowers.

In the past, country people grew their own food because they had to. Nowadays most of us do it from choice, both because gardening is a relaxation from the stresses of everyday life and also in a world where we are increasingly distant from our food producers it is nice to have a direct relationship with what we eat. Seasonal produce has become irrelevant in the global market, so the only way to recapture the thrill of the first fruits of summer is to grow your own, watching them form and picking them at the moment of perfect ripeness.

Establishing a kitchen garden theme for your containers is not difficult – simply by growing fruit and vegetables you are well on the way, and with the addition of characterful containers which echo the theme the picture will be complete. Strawberries and salad plants will grow quite happily in old baskets lined with moss or straw. Plant herbs in old pots or pans or even an old kettle; tin baths and buckets can be used for courgettes, squashes and tomatoes which need deep, fertile soil, and large tubs or barrels are ideal for large or tall-growing plants like climbing beans or artichokes. When growing climbing beans try to get hold of traditional bean poles, which are cut from coppiced wood, rather than the more usual canes. The irregular shape of bean poles is far more attractive and will make them a decorative feature in their own right. There was a time when bean poles and

LEFT: Every inch of this small terrace is used to create a flourishing kitchen garden.

TOP RIGHT: Discarded boxes from the greengrocer have been used to grow lettuces.

BOTTOM RIGHT: Surplus squashes make unusual and decorative containers.

pea sticks were readily obtainable, but now they are not so easy to find. You may be lucky enough to live in an area where woods are still managed traditionally, or even have your own hazel bushes which you can harvest, but if not, country fairs and gardening festivals sometimes have them for sale.

The back of the kitchen cupboard, the attic or the garden shed can often be a rich source of containers no longer used for their original purpose, or in the absence of your own junk you can look for other people's at car boot sales, house clearance sales and flea markets. Sometimes the most unlikely things can make successful containers. A metal grass-collecting box from an old mower can have drainage holes drilled in it so that it has a second lease of life as a container for mint or parsley, or straw-lined wooden fruit crates can be stacked in a group to create a layered garden filled with a variety of salad plants. Keep an open mind as you trawl your local junk shops.

A sunny, sheltered corner is ideal for your kitchen garden containers and in the absence of a rural setting they can be arranged against a backdrop of rustic fencing or woven-wattle fence panels, where they will look suitably countrified.

One of the main reasons that many of us choose to grow some of our own food is an increasing concern about modern agricultural methods with its intense use of chemical fertilizers, pesticides and herbicides. As allergies become more and more common many people have chosen to buy and grow organic foods – to return to the methods which have stood the test of time, where the soil itself is seen as something living, to be nurtured and fed so that it in turn will feed us. We used to laugh at the old gardeners who said 'the answer lies in the soil', but we have learnt, sometimes to our cost, that they were right, that healthy soil grows healthy plants which in turn help people to grow healthy.

To be truly organic requires quite a lot of effort initially, as you will need to mix your own compost. Potting composts are quite often marketed as organic, but unless they bear the symbol of one of the controlling organizations of organic growing such as the Soil Association this simply means that they contain composted manure which may well contain herbicides, pesticides or even hormones or antibiotics if it came

LEFT: *A fragrant chamomile seat is the perfect place to sit and admire your kitchen garden.*

OPPOSITE PAGE, LEFT: *Boxes of herbs can be stood in the sunniest spot in the garden and then carried indoors for harvesting.*

OPPOSITE PAGE, RIGHT: *Baskets make good containers for Mediterranean herbs which prefer free-draining soil.*

from conventional agriculture. To mix your own potting compost you need to start with good-quality loam, either from your own garden or bought by the bag from the garden centre. On its own loam is very heavy and can compact easily, so you will need to add humus. Traditionally peat was used for this purpose, but this is no longer advised as peat bog habitats are increasingly threatened by commercial extraction. Composted bark or cocoa fibre are recommended alternatives available at your local garden centre. Mix 2 parts loam with 2 parts humus and 1 part coarse grit for improved drainage. Pelleted organic chicken manure can also be added as a slow-release plant food – follow the manufacturers' recommendation for quantity.

If mixing up composts is far too complicated and labour-intensive for your liking, you can still improve the quality of your food by using commercially produced compost but cutting down on the use of chemical fertilizers and pesticides in your garden. An ordinary potting compost only contains sufficient fertilizer to last six weeks, after which it must be supplemented by liquid feeding or additional fertilizer. By mixing garden compost or composted manure into the potting compost you will improve its humus content and enrich it, and a layer of manure in the base of each container will encourage plants to grow strong healthy roots which will seek out this additional nourishment. Manure must never be used fresh, as it will burn

the plants. At the end of the season, provided there is no sign of pests or diseases, the soil can be sieved to remove excess root fibres, enriched with compost or manure and stacked or bagged ready for use next year.

You can make your own liquid feeds by filling a sack with composted manure, nettles or comfrey and suspending it in a water butt for at least six weeks. The resultant brews tend to be rather foul-smelling even when diluted and you may prefer to buy a liquid seaweed feed which is a lot more pleasant to use, but read the label carefully as some have added chemical fertilizers. During the growing season use liquid feeds at least once a fortnight. For gross feeders such as tomatoes and courgettes once a week is recommended.

Keeping pests at bay is particularly important in the kitchen garden. In the flower garden they are merely unsightly, but with edible crops you certainly don't want to find that you are sharing your meal with a couple of caterpillars or a slimy slug. When it comes to food crops you really should try to avoid chemical pesticides, which can leave harmful residues on the plants – it is far better to use old-fashioned methods of pest control or natural predators.

Slugs and snails are among the most destructive of garden pests. Tender young salad plants will disappear overnight and larger plants soon lose their appeal when crisscrossed with snail trails and disfigured by large holes. Visit your container garden at dusk and use a torch to locate the pests as they emerge for their evening feast. How you dispose of them is up to you, but a swift end is the most merciful. Encourage hedgehogs, frogs and toads into your garden and you will find that they take over the task of evening patrol as slugs and snails are numbered among their favourite delicacies.

Caterpillars cause most damage to members of the brassica family, which includes cabbages, broccoli and cauliflowers, but you are unlikely to grow these in containers. On other plants the numbers are likely to be small and they can be picked off by hand.

Greenfly are ever-present in the garden, especially after a mild winter. A good population of ladybirds will keep them under control, but where there is a bad infestation you can spray the plant with soapy water or use a natural insecticide such as derris, which is derived from the pyrethrum daisy. Unfortunately derris does not discriminate between friend and foe and will also kill ladybirds, hoverflies and any other insect it touches.

The vine weevil is a pest which has been encouraged by modern commercial horticulture. It thrives in the peat-based composts that growers use and unless they employ frequent chemical controls these pests survive to wreak havoc in our gardens. Usually the first sign that you have a problem is that a plant begins to wilt and when you examine it the whole plant lifts away in your hand because the vine weevil grub has eaten most of the root system. Once it has colonized a container your best bet is to bag up the compost and dispose of it and then wash the container thoroughly before starting again with fresh compost.

Blackfly can be a nuisance in the vegetable garden, particularly on beans. It has long been common practice to grow nasturtiums nearby as the blackfly find them even more attractive than beans, but there is a danger that they may simply act as an additional lure. Soapy water or derris is probably a better bet.

Whitefly thrive in greenhouses and conservatories and are less of a problem

outdoors. If you have a serious infestation in the garden you could try a particularly ingenious solution. Coat a

large piece of card with petroleum jelly, give the infected plants a quick shake and as the whitefly take to the air wave the card around – you will catch the whitefly by the hundreds. Children find this very enjoyable!

ABOVE: *Bright flowers in the kitchen attract bees and other beneficial insects. The French marigold is reputed to keep whitefly at bay.*

Kitchen-garden containers overflowing with delicious fruit and vegetables look even better when edible flowers are included. The eating of flowers was commonplace in Elizabethan England, when many were used as flavourings in food and to make syrups and cordials. Violets, roses, cowslips, primroses and gillyflowers (pinks) were commonly used ingredients. Throughout the intervening centuries the popularity of edible flowers has waxed and waned. Now that the subject of food is fashionable and young chefs are celebrities, flowers once again appear on our plates and even supermarkets sell packs of edible flowers alongside rocket, lamb's lettuce and lollo rosso.

Nasturtiums are among the best-known, with their brilliant colours and their delicious peppery flavour which will enhance any salad. They are also one of the easiest of all flowers to grow; simply push the seed into the soil where it will germinate quickly and then all you have to do is watch them grow. Blackfly can be a problem – at the first sign of an infestation treat the plants with soapy water and be sure to always wash flowers thoroughly before you use them, just in case there are a few lurking inside. Grow climbing varieties among runner beans, or use bush nasturtiums to edge containers.

Pansies with their beautifully marked faces look wonderful in salads or frosted on cakes or desserts. Plant them among lettuces in the kitchen garden to create a pretty contrast of foliage and flowers. Keep the plants blooming by picking the flowers as soon as they reach maturity and be sure to deadhead any which you may have missed before they set seed. If the plants get 'leggy' cut them back by about half to stimulate a new flush of flowers.

The pot marigold (*Calendula officinalis*) was traditionally used as a colouring and flavouring for stews, cakes and puddings, a cheap substitute for saffron, but nowadays individual petals are scattered on dishes as decoration. Like nasturtiums, pot marigolds are very easy to grow. They can be interplanted among your vegetables or grown in individual pots. Deadhead them regularly to ensure a continuing supply of flowers.

Pinks, once known as gillyflowers, were important flavourings in the Middle Ages, used in food but more importantly in drinks, where they were employed to flavour wines and ales. Nowadays pinks are really only used as frosted or candied decorations for cakes and desserts, as the flavour is a bit too perfumed for modern tastes.

Chives are grown for their foliage, but their pretty flowers are highly decorative and if divided up into individual florets they can be scattered on salads. Use the flowers when they are fully open. After flowering cut the chive plant back to near ground level to encourage new growth and a second flush of flowers.

LEFT: *An old tin bath filled with rich compost will yield a good crop of courgettes from just a single plant.*

BELOW: *The pot marigold was once used as a cheap substitute for saffron.*

There is an old saying that 'a garden without borage is a garden without courage', so for this reason alone it should probably be included in your garden, but there are other good reasons: the lovely blue star flowers are the finishing touch to a summer glass of Pimms and their delicate cucumber flavour is a delicious addition to a fruit salad. Borage is even richer in gamma linolenic acid than evening primrose, so its regular use could also have health benefits. Borage (*Borago officinalis*) grows readily from seed.

Growing fruit in containers is surprisingly easy provided you choose your varieties carefully. Obviously this type of cultivation is not suited to every fruit, but there are sufficient that will do well enough to provide you with some tasty treats from your kitchen-garden containers. Even dwarf fruit trees grow surprisingly well in a large pot and most garden centres have a selection of these plants, which are raised specifically for container cultivation.

The most obvious choice of fruit is the strawberry, which often does better grown in a tub, barrel or specially designed strawberry pot than it does grown in the ground, where it can suffer from slug damage and is also more prone to mildew. One of the advantages of growing strawberries in freestanding containers is that they are easy to protect from birds by covering them with netting.

Different varieties of strawberries bear fruit at different times of year, so if you are clever with your choice you can enjoy two or three crops. Interplant with wild strawberries and you will be picking fruit all summer, although sometimes it may be little more than a delicious morsel. To keep the plants cropping well, cut back the foliage after fruiting and feed with a high-potash plant food. The plants will crop prolifically for three years, after which they should be replaced with young plants. These can be rooted from

OPPOSITE: *Culinary herbs are at their best before they begin to flower. Regular harvesting encourages continued strong growth.*

RIGHT: *Pink-flowered strawberries are more decorative than productive but can be included among other strawberry plants for a splash of colour.*

runners produced by the parent plant. Simply use a hairpin or a bent piece of wire to pin a plantlet onto the surface of the compost in a small pot placed near the parent plant. When it has rooted the runner can be detached.

Soft fruit bushes – redcurrants, whitecurrants, blackcurrants and gooseberries – will all grow in a large container when planted in a rich loam-based compost, but they can look rather unattractive except for the brief period when they are laden with ripening fruit. If any of these fruit is a favourite it is still worth including in your kitchen garden just for the pleasure of eating the fruit straight from the bush. With the exception of the blackcurrant they can be trained into standards which are more attractive-looking plants. To do this, buy a young plant with a strong main stem. Trim sideshoots back to the main stem, but leave in place any bunches of foliage growing direct from the main stem. When the main stem reaches the desired height, cut back the growing tip to the first leaf joint to encourage it to branch. As these new branches reach 15cm (6in) long, cut out the growing tips once more and your plant will quickly establish the bushy

head of a standard. At this stage you can remove the foliage from the main stem. Alternatively, you may be able to buy a trained standard from a specialist fruit nursery. Regular topdressing with bonemeal and composted manure or pelleted chicken manure will ensure that your fruit bush crops well.

No kitchen garden is complete without herbs. One of the most

attractive ways to grow them is in a large half-barrel with a standard bay tree as the centrepiece. Surround the tree with a selection of your favourite herbs. Chives, parsley and annuals such as dill, chervil, rocket and coriander are good choices, but avoid mint as it is very invasive. Be sure to give an organic liquid feed regularly as the herbs will have to compete with the bay tree.

New Rustic

New Rustic combines the informality and simple materials of traditional rustic style with stunning plants and vibrant paint colours to give containers a contemporary country look which will appeal to the new generation of style-conscious gardeners.

UNTIL THE LATE 19th century 'rustic' gardens just happened – the country gardener simply put plants together in pleasing combinations wherever there was space among the vegetables, along the edge of paths and in a miscellany of containers clustered around the kitchen door and the front porch.

The concept of designing a garden was left to the aristocracy and the landed gentry. The aristocracy favoured design on a grand scale where plants were very much secondary to the carefully landscaped terraces edged with magnificent urns, the lakes, the formal walks and the statuary. The gentry favoured a scaled-down version of the aristocratic garden, although plants were more central to the design. This style of gardening is still thriving in some parks and municipal gardens, where annual bedding plants are regimented in violently colourful displays of breathtaking vulgarity.

It was William Robinson who first introduced informality into garden design when he advocated the use of wildflowers in gardens. He was an Irishman of strongly held opinions which he never failed to express. He loathed gardens designed, as he put it, by 'builders and wallpaper merchants' with their 'fountainmongery'. He considered geometrically shaped flower beds filled with carpet bedding to be an eyesore, referring to them as 'pastry-cook's work', and he believed that carpet bedding was degrading to individual plants.

Robinson wrote two hugely influential books, *The English Flower Garden* and *The Wild Garden*. In the latter he recommended a style of gardening which is still the epitome of all that is finest in English country gardening – a garden where the cultivated areas are a gentle interpretation of the countryside beyond rather than a stark contrast to it.

Since William Robinson's time a new generation of 'wildflowers' has been developed. These are plants which are somewhere between the original native plants and the full-blown cultivated varieties, giving gardeners reliable plants which still retain their informal charm.

LEFT: *Once introduced to the garden California poppies (*Eschscholzia*) will self-seed anywhere.*

RIGHT: *The pinky-brown paintwork on the Versailles tub perfectly matches the flowers of* **Phygelius** *'Winchester Fanfare'.*

Craft Project 10

VERSAILLES TUB

YOU WILL NEED

- 4 corner posts, 50mm (2in) square by 375mm (15in) long
- 8 planks of timber, 150mm (6in) wide by 25mm (1in) thick by 325mm (13in) long
- 8 × 300mm (12in) lengths of 25mm (1in) square batten
- 2 × 275mm (11in) lengths of 25mm (1in) square batten
- 4 × 375mm (15in) lengths of 50 × 25mm (2 × 1in) batten
- 50mm (2in) wood screws
- 40mm (1½in) nails
- 4 × 75mm (3in) lengths of 13mm (½in) dowel
- 4 large pine cones
- Hand saw
- Electric drill and 13mm (½in) bit
- Hammer
- Screwdriver

A PLANT TUB associated with one of the great formal gardens of Europe is given a rustic interpretation.

Construction

1. Screw two 25mm (1in) square battens to each corner post as shown, using 50mm (2in) wood screws.

2. Assemble the front and back panels in turn by laying two corner posts on your work surface with the fixed battens facing one another. Rest two planks on the battens and secure with 40mm (1½in) nails. Nail one 275mm (11in) long batten along the bottom of each lower plank.

3. Join the back and front on each side by standing the panels on end on the work surface with their remaining battens facing one another. Nail two further planks to each pair of battens. Rest the four lengths of 50 × 25mm (2 × 1in) batten on the base supports and nail in place.

3. Paint the tub inside and out and leave to dry.

4. To make the pine cone finials, drill a 13mm (½in) hole centrally in each corner post. Squeeze a little wood glue into the hole and push in a length of dowel, leaving 40mm (1½in) proud. Drill a hole in the base of each cone, glue the holes and push each cone firmly onto a protruding dowel.

TO DECORATE

- Water-based preservative wood stain or satin finish paint
- Paintbrush
- Waterproof wood glue

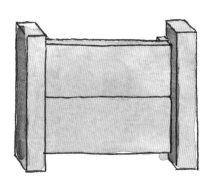

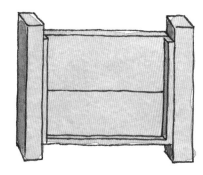

1. *Position of battens on corner posts.*

2. *Front (exterior) view of panel.*

3. *Back (interior) view of panel.*

Looking After Your Versailles Tub

All wooden garden furniture will last longer if it can be stored under cover during the winter. To keep the colours vibrant, repaint the tubs each spring.

An Extra Dimension

The pine cone finials don't just look good – they forecast the weather as well, opening wide in dry conditions and closing right up in the damp.

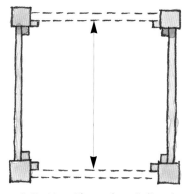

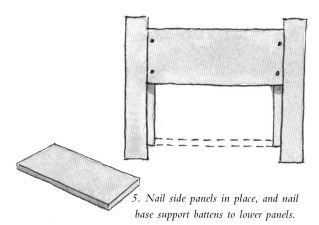

4. *Position side panels as indicated.*

5. *Nail side panels in place, and nail base support battens to lower panels.*

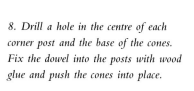

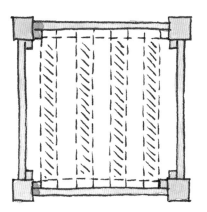

6. *Nail base battens to the support battens, evenly spaced along them.*

7. *View of completed tub from above.*

8. *Drill a hole in the centre of each corner post and the base of the cones. Fix the dowel into the posts with wood glue and push the cones into place.*

IMPRESSIONIST PLANTS

Fashions come and go in gardening, but planting in drifts of colour is no passing fad. The favoured style of Gertrude Jekyll, that most influential of gardeners, it persists long after her time and remains a staple of English gardens.

William Robinson was not enthusiastic about fashionable new plants introduced to English gardens from abroad, preferring to draw on hardy herbaceous plants which were native or long-established in Britain and which he knew would grow reliably. These are still the foundation of this style of planting, which mixes hardy plants in an impressionistic blend of colours.

Gertrude Jekyll was an enthusiastic supporter of Robinson's style of gardening. She had the sense of colour of an artist and the instincts of a natural gardener, observing the effects which the Impressionist painters achieved by blending many shades to create the impression of a single colour. With the architect Edwin Luytens she toured the lanes of Surrey to learn from the cottage gardens. She loved their simplicity and relished the softening effect that time had on gardens, where walls were smothered by tumbling flowers and paths were colonized by creeping plants.

Gertrude Jekylll used wild plants in her gardens but much of her

Aster × frikartii 'Jungfrau'

Lavandula angustifolia 'Hidcote'

planting drew on plants of Mediterranean origin such as lavender, cistus, rosemary and sages with their silvery-grey foliage and hazy colours. However, it was the broad sweep of colour rather than the individual plants which characterized a style which is enduringly popular. Her gardens moved from one area of colour to another and this is a principle which can be applied to any area of planting, however large or small. The plants listed here are a starting point around which you can build a collection of colour-themed hardy plants for your New Rustic containers.

PINKS, BLUES AND PURPLES

A group of containers planted in these colours will blend pleasingly from a distance and it is only when you get closer that the different colours will become apparent. *Geranium* is a vast genus of hardy plants with many different flower colours. *G. macrorrhizum* 'Ingwersen's Variety' has soft pink flowers and light green foliage which develops good autumn colour. *G.* 'Johnson's Blue' bears clear blue flowers in abundance and *G. phaeum*, known as 'the mourning widow' has small deep purply-black flowers and a loose habit. On its own it is not very impressive, but as a foil to other plants in its colour range it is ideal. Geraniums do well in full sun or partial shade and grow in most soils.

Erigeron karvinskianus is a delightful container plant which will seed itself in every nook and cranny, softening the garden with its long-lasting display of delicate daisies which open white and deepen from pale to deep pink. There are also larger varieties of erigeron which bear large flowers from mid-spring to late summer. *E.* 'Dunkelste Aller' has very dark blue flowers and *E* 'Charity' has clear pink. All are easy to grow.

The aster with its blue daisy flowers brings autumn colour to the garden. The smaller varieties will do well in containers, but be careful to select mildew-resistant

Erigeron 'Dunkelste Aller'

Geranium 'Johnson's Blue'

varieties such as *Aster novi-belgii* 'Royal Velvet' or *A.* × *frikartii*.

Plants with coloured foliage will help to add depth to the colour scheme. *Heuchera micrantha* var. *diversifolia* 'Palace Purple' or *H.* 'Chocolate Ruffles' have deep pinky-purple and pinky-brown foliage and dainty sprigs of tiny bell flowers.

Lavender is an essential component of the New Rustic garden. Prune it after flowering to maintain a pleasing rounded shape. The compact forms are best suited for container growing. *Lavandula angustifolia* 'Hidcote' with silvery foliage and deepest blue flowers reaches a height of 30cm (12in) and spread of 45cm (18in). *L. a.* 'Munstead' is slightly taller but also has good deep blue flowers. *L. stoechas* (French lavender) with its flaring petals looks quite different from other lavenders, while *L. s.* 'Helmsdale' has attractive deep purple flowerheads. A recent development is an annual lavender,

Helenium 'Wyndley'

'Lady', which can be grown from seed or bought as young plants. Its loose habit makes it ideal for hanging baskets and containers. All lavenders need a sunny site and free-draining soil with added grit. If they have been grown in peat, be sure to soak the plant and loosen the rootball when transplanting.

REDS, YELLOWS, ORANGES

A hot, sunny corner is the ideal position for a group of containers planted with 'hot' colours. Make sure you include plenty of yellows as this lifts and intensifies the reds, which can lose definition when grouped together.

The flowers of the day-lily (*Hemerocallis*) last for only one day, but they are borne prolifically in the summer and the strap-like foliage is attractive before and after flowering. *H.* 'Corky' is a compact variety of 45cm (18in) height and spread which does well

in a container. The red-hot poker (*Kniphofia*) is another plant which, in its miniature form, does well in containers. *K.* 'Little Maid' has pale creamy yellow flower spikes reaching 45cm (18in) above grass-like foliage and *K. triangularis* has small red flowers in the autumn. Plant in well-drained soil.

Achilleas come in a range of colours from palest creamy yellow to vibrant reds and all will do well in a hot dry position. *Achillea* 'Moonshine' is one of the best known with flat heads of bright yellow flowers throughout the summer, but *A.* 'Lachsschönheit' and *A. millefolium* 'Paprika' are worth considering. *Geum* 'Lady Stratheden' has clear yellow flowers and *G.* 'Mrs J. Bradshaw' is one of the purest scarlet flowers in the garden. *Helenium* 'Bressingham Gold' has pure yellow flowers, those of *H.* 'Wyndley' are orange and *H.* 'Riverton Gem' is red and gold. They need regular division in spring or autumn to perform well.

Achillea millefolium 'Paprika'

The original rustic gardens had little or no money spent on them; they were planted with flowers collected from the wild, cuttings given by neighbours and plants grown from home-collected seed. Containers and plant supports were fashioned from twigs, vines and branches cut from hedges and coppiced woodland. When William Robinson popularized this style of gardening, nurserymen and craftsmen saw a commercial opportunity and took it up with great enthusiasm. Nurseries collected wildflowers and produced improved strains and colour variations, while craftsmen became expert at erecting rustic arbours, arches, pergolas and summerhouses. Books were written devoted entirely to the subject of rustic style and there was a time in the late 19th century when no fashionable garden was to be seen without an area given over to rusticity.

In recent years there has been a renaissance in the use of rustic materials in the garden as it is recognized that although they may not be as durable as modern materials they are far more sympathetic to their surroundings and even their slow disintegration has charm. It is no longer difficult to buy woven willow or hazel plant supports and many garden centres now sell fence panels woven from twigs alongside the more usual fencing. Country fairs, garden shows and agricultural shows usually have at least one craftsman or

ABOVE: *A short-stemmed variety of sunflower retains its inherent beauty while being better suited to pot cultivation.*

RIGHT: *An old manger is a wonderfully rustic container for a vivid display of yellow rudbeckia.*

woman making rustic items and real enthusiasts can go on courses and learn how to weave their own.

Giving your garden a rustic theme is really quite simple, combining as it does relaxed informal planting and containers made from natural materials. New Rustic uses all these, but adds a modern interpretation with more vibrant flowers, combined at times with bright

paint colours used in colour washes or distressed paint finishes on some of the containers.

In the spirit of the original rustic gardeners you should first look through your shed, garage or attic to find anything which might be used as a container. Don't worry if its life will be limited outdoors – it will be more useful in the garden than it is gathering dust in a corner. An old laundry hamper or a picnic basket lined with moss or even old carpet felt and planted with a selection of perennials will last four or five years in the garden before it needs to be replaced. A log basket with broken handles can be used in place of a large pot to hold a climbing rose underplanted with hardy geraniums or filled with a selection of lavenders. Don't be too purist about it, though – the original rustic gardener would not have discarded something because it wasn't made from the correct materials. For example, a distressed paint finish can turn a modern wooden window box into an aged relic and a length of vine woven through the wirework of a hanging basket before it is planted will give it a rustic look.

Rustic poles for arches, pergolas and plant supports can be bought at most garden centres, where some are even available as kits ready for self-assembly. However, the most economical way to buy them is from a timbermill or woodyard, where you will also get a better choice.

Although some styles of garden transplant well into any setting, some do not, and this generally includes the rustic garden. Its natural setting is the countryside, with the plants and structures blending harmoniously with the view beyond. When this style of gardening was taken up by William Robinson he too stressed the importance of relating the garden to its surroundings. This is not to say that you must live in the depths of the country, but it does mean that to work well your garden should have green boundaries or greenery beyond or it may look as contrived as the 'pastry cook work' and 'fountainmongery' that William Robinson so despised.

The importance of house and garden relating to one another are wonderfully described by a contemporary of William Robinson called James Shirley Hibberd. He wrote what is to modern tastes an extraordinary book called *Rustic* *Adornments for Homes of Taste*, a book full of hilarious advice and ghastly excesses, but even he knew it was possible to go too far; he says, 'Nothing can be more absurd than to imitate eastern luxury in carpets and furniture, and by one step pass from mirrors and gilt cornices, and rich tapestry, to honeysuckle hedges, hermits' huts and bogs covered with toadstools.'

In garden design the house, the boundaries and the view beyond are

OPPOSITE PAGE: *By selecting colourful containers and keeping twigs and rustic poles to a minimum, this style of garden can work in an urban setting.*

BELOW, LEFT: *A brightly painted ladder makes an unusual plant stand.*

BELOW, RIGHT: *A tabletop display draws the eye and allows you to appreciate the beauty of flowers which may otherwise go unnoticed.*

integral parts of the whole picture which must be taken into account if the finished garden is to be really successful. If the view over the fence is a delight everything in the garden should complement and draw the eye towards that view; if on the other hand there is no view or it is dominated by an ugly feature, the garden itself should have a strong focal point which will keep the eye within the garden. In a garden with a good outlook use the containers, the plants and rustic supports to frame the view by placing them either side of the garden so that the eye travels past them and makes the view part of the garden. Any groups of containers placed centrally in the garden should be at a low level so that once again the eye travels over them and on to the view beyond.

This may all sound rather large scale when related to containers, but a good view does not necessarily mean rolling open countryside or mountains – it can be a pretty tree in the garden next door or a climbing rose on the boundary fence. The scale is different but the principle is the same.

If you are determined to have a rustic garden in spite of urban surroundings, the good news is that New Rustic can still work provided you are restrained in its interpretation. Concentrate more on brightly painted containers and keep rustic twigs and poles out of the picture except as occasional plant supports. Informal planting with hardy perennials and a few annuals to provide additional colour will give a country feel to an urban garden without turning it into a theme park.

There is a tendency to think of container planting as something which is done anew each year with old plants rooted up, discarded and replaced by new young plants. The mixed planting of the New Rustic garden offers the more adventurous container gardener a more interesting alternative to the usual pattern of spring bulbs followed by bedding plants. Experiment with mixtures of old-fashioned favourites such as southernwood (*Artemisia abrotanum*) planted with newer plants such as pink cow parsley (*Chaerophyllum hirsutum* 'Roseum'), pink and white varieties of *Lychnis coronaria* and the trailing pink marguerite *Argyranthemum* 'Flamingo'. Group them with other containers featuring plants in the same colour range, some more intense such as *Heuchera* 'Chocolate Ruffles' and *Anthriscus sylvestris* 'Ravenswing' with its sombre black foliage and some paler, such as *Eryngium giganteum* 'Silver Ghost' (a biennial, but it self-seeds readily) or *Astrantia major* subsp. *involucrata* 'Shaggy' with its soft pinky-green flowers. The idea is to build a complete picture from its component parts, and you will need to step back regularly to check on your progress and adjust the colouring.

Never be afraid to learn from the experts. Visit the great garden shows and even minor ones to see what is new, tear out pictures which inspire you from newspapers and magazines and obtain catalogues from specialist nurseries which grow interesting herbaceous plants. When you are gardening on a small scale you can afford to be selective, and anyway it is fun to search out an elusive plant.

It is possible to grow even quite large plants in pots for many years with only occasional repotting. Provided they are topdressed annually with a mulch of rich compost and watered regularly during the growing season with a liquid feed once a fortnight or so, they should grow as well as in the border. However, it is probably best to restrict yourself to lower-growing varieties unless you have some really large containers, because a plant four times the height of its container looks out of proportion with its surroundings unless it is a climber.

To continue flowering well, herbaceous plants need to be divided roughly every three years. Generally the growth on the outside of a clump is the most vigorous while the centre is often rather woody and should be discarded. Container-grown plants are more vulnerable to the cold than those in the border, so resist cutting them right back in the autumn – cut back by half at the most. Remove plant saucers from under pots in autumn and try to raise containers slightly off the ground to ensure that they drain freely – waterlogging kills more hardy plants than cold does.

RIGHT: *If well cared for, this basket of achilleas and sedums will not need replanting for three years.*

Traditionally the rustic garden used natural materials in their natural subtle shades. New Rustic introduces bright colours which bring a fresh vigour to this style of gardening. The emphasis is still on materials which occur naturally in the garden: willow and hazel shoots thrown up after winter coppicing, grape vines and the twining stems of climbing honeysuckle or Russian vine cut down in the annual round of pruning, twigs collected from hedges and shrubs and prunings from fruit trees. However, when used alongside brightly painted containers the effect is much livelier. Don't be afraid to use strong colours – lime, violet and turquoise are some of the colours in the New Rustic palette which will transform simple wooden containers into stylish planters. Use two or more colours applied roughly so that the finish is suitably rustic. Part of the charm of this type of paint effect is that it fades over time and you can either leave it to soften slowly or add a new coat of paint each year in a different colour so that gradually it achieves a wonderful depth of impressionistic colour. You can use any type of water-based paint or wood stain. Plant supports and rustic trellis can also be painted, but be careful not to get too carried away or the garden will begin to look like a fairground. Any painted colour introduced to the garden should be to enhance the flowers rather than detract from them.

When planting painted containers you have the choice of choosing flowers in harmonious or contrasting shades and depending on which you choose you can create very different effects. Pink, purple and violet flowers planted in a container painted in shades of blue and purple may use intense colours but they

will blend harmoniously; plant the same container with flowers in the contrasting colours of orange and yellow and the result will have real drama. Once again it is important not to do this too much or it becomes wearying rather than exciting.

Colour is a fascinating subject and we respond to it emotionally as well as visually. You can make use of this in the garden by creating strong dramatic effects which incorporate your favourite colours. When you visit art galleries observe how the artists have used colour and how you respond to it, especially the great colourists such as Monet and Bonnard. Buy postcards of the pictures which particularly appeal to you and use them as colour references for your planting. Alternatively, look at the books of contemporary designers Tricia Guild and Kaffe Fassett, both of whom have a wonderful feeling for colour. Tricia Guild's *Painted Country* is New Rustic at its best. This may all seem rather excessive when all you are wanting to do is plant up a couple of pots, and if you have a natural feel for colour you can trust your instincts. However, if you are afraid to use colour boldly and tend towards the safer options which are reliable but not very exciting it will give you confidence.

OPPOSITE: *A brightly painted barrel filled with vivid ranunculus has real eye-catching impact.*

RIGHT: *The sherbet colours of Iceland poppies* (Papaver nudicaule) *are brought into relief by the weathered background.*

The New Rustic garden is a garden for all seasons; even in winter the natural materials which form its framework remain interesting to look at and they can be enhanced by seasonal planting. Native wildflowers and their cultivars are particularly appropriate in the winter and spring. Choose snowdrop and aconites for the earliest months of the year, planted in little baskets and emerging through a bed of moss. Follow these with scented *Iris reticulata* and crocus. Avoid the striped or very large-flowered crocuses and plant a single variety in each container if you want the feel of a wild garden, otherwise go for big and bold.

With the arrival of spring many of the woodland wildflowers such as primroses, cowslips, violets, wood anemones and bluebells should have a place in the rustic garden. If the colours are a bit too subtle for New Rustic you can select modern cultivars with stronger colours. Barnhaven primulas, a polyanthus-type primula, are familiar to gardeners the world over and renowned for the jewel-like colours of the flowers, their sweet scent and their hardiness. A group of painted containers individually planted with deep blue primulas, *Viola* 'Freckles' with its white face dotted with blue, sky-blue wood anemones and bluebells will have plenty of impact. Alternatively,

LEFT: *A wicker hamper overflowing with Impressionist flowers gives a neglected shed the air of a rural retreat.*

you could choose a pink and white colour theme with pink double-flowered primulas, pink bluebells, white wood anemones and white or pale lavender violets. In a rural setting it is generally best to stick with the colours nature prefers, but in an urban New Rustic garden where the plants don't need to relate to the larger landscape it can be fun to experiment.

There is a wealth of choice for the summer with many hardy perennials suitable for container growing, but do include plants which will continue to give good value in the autumn. Late-flowering hardy plants include Michaelmas daisies and *Aster lateriflorus* 'Horizontalis' is a particularly good choice, with tiny leaves which take on a coppery-purple hue in September contrasting with the very small lilac flowers. It reaches a height of 60cm (2ft) and a spread of 45cm (18in). *A. novi-belgii* 'Professor Anton Kippenberg' has clear blue flowers and is a compact plant with a height of 30cm (12in) and a spread of 45cm (18in). Sedum's fleshy leaves and immature flowerheads look good from midsummer onwards, but it comes into its full glory in the autumn when its dusky-rose flowers open fully. Choose a low-growing variety such as *Sedum* 'Ruby Glow' with its purply-red foliage and crimson flowers. *Liriope muscari* is another good choice for the New Rustic autumn garden, with narrow, glossy green leaves and spikes of thickly clustered purple flowers.

SUPPLIERS

Garden antiques and collectibles
Nakota Curios
Courthouse Street
Hastings Old Town
TN34 3ES
tel 01424 438900

and

Hastings Antique Centre
59–61 Norman Road
St Leonards on Sea
E. Sussex
TN38 0EG
tel: 01424 428561
and the many antique and bric-a-brac shops of Hastings Old Town as well as from the author's and photographer's own collections.

Plants
Merriments Nursery
Hawkhurst Road
Hurst Green, E. Sussex TN19 7RA
tel: 01580 860666

Country Gardens Nursery
Bexhill
Hastings, E. Sussex
TN38 8AR
tel: 01424 443414

Harborough Nursery
Guestling Thorne
Nr Hastings, E. Sussex TN35 4LU
tel: 01424 814220

Potting compost
Levington Horticulture

Rustic baskets
English Hurdle
Curload
Stoke St Gregory
Taunton
Somerset TA3 6JD
tel: 01823 698418

Rustic willow and wood props
Terrace & Garden
Orchard House
Patmore End
Ugley
Bishop's Stortford
Herts CM22 6JA
tel: 01799 543289
(mail order)

Farmyard and florist's buckets
Garden Trading Company
Unit 9 Wychwood Business Centre
Shipton under Wychwood
Oxon OX7 6XU
tel: 01993 832200
(mail order)

American Folk Art props
Appalachia
14a George Street
St Albans
Herts AL3 4ER
tel: 01727 836796

Trugs and planters
Somerset Creative Products
Laurel Farm
Westham
Wedmore
Somerset BS28 4UZ
tel: 01934 712416

Glazed terracotta pots on pages 16–17
The Brooke Pottery
Cottisbrooke, Northampton
tel: 01604 505886

Handmade terracotta pots
Whichford Pottery
Whichford, Nr Shipton on Stour
Warks CV36 5PG
tel: 01608 684416

Decoupage
Linda Talmage
46 Market Place, Brackley
Northants NN13 7DP
tel: 01280 701233

Mediterranean paints on page 10
Brats Paints
281 Kings Road
London SW3 5EW
tel: 0171 351 7674

Shells
Marine Arts Ltd
The Shell Factory
Long Rock
Penzance
Cornwall
TR20 8HX
tel: 01736 365169
(wholesale shells & marine only)

Specialist nurseries
UNITED KINGDOM
Pelargoniums
The National Pelargonium Collection
Fibrex Nurseries
Honeybourne Road
Pebworth
Stratford-upon-Avon
Warks CV37 8XT
tel: 01789 720788

The Vernon Geranium Nursery,
Cuddington Way
Cheam
Sutton, Surrey SM2 7JB
tel: 0181 393 7616

Herbaceous Perennials
Merriments Nursery
Hawkhurst Road
Hurst Green, E. Sussex TN19 7RA
tel: 01580 860666

Great Dixter Nurseries
Northiam
Rye, E. Sussex TN31 6PH
Tel: 01797 253107

Bressingham Gardens
Bressingham
Diss, Norfolk IP22 2AB
tel: 0379 88464

Hostas
Goldbrook Plants
Hoxne
Eye, Suffolk IP21 5AN
tel: 01379 668770

The Hosta Garden
47 Birch Grove
London W3 9SP
tel: 0181 248 1300

Bulbs
Avon Bulbs
Burnt House Farm
Mid Lambrook, South Petherton
Somerset TA13 5HE
tel: 01460 242177

Jacques Amand Ltd
The Nurseries
145 Clamp Hill
Stanmore
Middx HA7 3JS
tel: 0181 393 4265

Broadleigh Gardens
Bishops Hull
Taunton, Somerset TA4 1AE
01823 286231

Hardy Geraniums
Glebe Cottage Plants
Pixie Lane
Warkleigh
Umberleigh, Devon EX37 9DH
tel: 01769 540554

Craigieburn Classic Plants
Craigieburn House, by Moffat,
Dumfries DG10 9LF
tel: 01683 221250

Conservatory Plants
Conservatory Plantline
West Bergholt
Colchester, Essex CO6 3DH
tel: 01206 242 533

Newington Nurseries
Bathway Farm
Chewton Mendip, Somerset BA3 4LN
tel: 01761 241 283

Roses
David Austin Roses
Bowling Green Lane
Albrighton
Wolverhampton
W. Midlands WV7 3HB
tel: 01902 373 931

Just Roses
Beales Lane
Northiam
Nr Rye, E. Sussex TN31 6QY
tel: 01797 252355

Grasses
Green Farm Plants
Bury Court
Bentley
Farnham, Surrey GU10 5JX
tel: 01420 23202

Beth Chatto Gardens Ltd
Elmstead Market
Colchester
Essex CO7 7DB
tel: 01206 822007

Ferns
Fibrex Nurseries Ltd
Honeybourne Road
Pebworth
Stratford-upon-Avon
Warks CV37 8XT
tel: 01789 720788

Rickard's Hardy Ferns,
Kyre Park
Kyre
Tenbury Wells, Worcs WR15 8RP
tel: 01885 410282

Herbs
Iden Croft Herbs
Frittenden Road
Staplehurst
Kent, TN12 0DH
tel: 01580 891432

Hollington Nurseries
Woolton Hill
Newbury, Berks RG20 9XT
tel: 01635 253908

Citrus
Read's Nursery
Hales Hall
Loddon, Norfolk
NR14 6QW
tel: 01508 548395

The Citrus Centre
West Mare Lane
Marehill
Pulborough, W. Sussex RH20 2EA
tel: 01798 872786

Auriculas
Brenda Hyatt
1 Toddington Crescent
Bluebell Hill
Nr Chatham, Kent
ME5 9QT
tel: 01634 863251

Philip Hocking
12 Lambrook Close
Taunton, Somerset TA10 9EZ
tel: 01823 332730

NORTH AMERICA
Pelargoniums
Wheeler Farm Gardens
171 Bartlett Street
Portland, CT 06480

Herbaceous Perennials
White Flower Farm
Litchfield
CT 06759-0050
tel: 800 503 9624

Bluestone Perennials
7239 Middle Ridge Road
Madison
Ohio 44057
tel: 800 852 5243

Hostas
Daylily Farms & Nursery
RT1 Box 89A
Bakersville NC28705

Goods Nursery
P O Box 701482
51225 Ann Arbor Road
Plymouth, MI 48170-0965

Bulbs
John Scheepers Inc.
23 Tulip Drive
Bantam, CT 06750
tel: 860 567 0838

Hardy Geraniums
Busse Gardens
5873 Oliver Avenue., SW.
Cokato, MN 55321-4229
tel: 800 544 3192

Canyon Creek Nursery
3527 Dry Creek Road
Oroville, CA 95965
tel: 916 533 2166

Conservatory Plants
Logee's Greenhouses
141 North Street
Danielson CT 06239
tel: 860 774 8038

Plumeria People
910 Leander Drive
Leander, TX 78641

Roses
Heirloom Old Garden Roses
24062 Riverside Drive
St Paul, OR 97137
tel: 503 538 1576

The Antique Rose Emporium
9300 Lueckmeyer Road
Brenham, TX 77833
tel: 800 441 0002

Grasses
Shady Oaks Nursery
112 10th Ave. SE.,
Waseca, MN 56093
Tel: 800 504 8006

Limerock Ornamental Grasses Inc.
70 Sawmill Road
Port Matilda, PA 16870
tel: 814 692 2272

Ferns
Shady Oaks Nursery
112 10th Avenue SE., Dept. FG
Waseca, MN 56093
Tel: 800 504 8006

Native Plants
Busse Gardens
5873 Oliver Avenue SW.
Cokato, MN 55321-4229
tel: 800 544 3192

WE-DU Nurseries
RR5 Box 724
Marion, NC 28752-9338

Pine Ridge Gardens
832F Sycamore Road
London AR 72847

Herbs
Sandy Mush Herb Nursery
316 Surrett Cove Road
Leicester, NC28748-5517

The Thyme Garden
20546 Alsea Hwy
Alsea, OR 97324

Citrus
Four Winds Growers
P.O. Box 3538
Fremont, CA 94539
tel: 510 656 2591

INDEX

Page numbers in *italics* refer to picture captions